The Seasonal Flower Grower

The Seasonal Flower Grower

A calendar of monthly tasks for a beautiful
and fragrant garden

Jonathan Edwards
and Peter McHoy

southwater

This edition is published by Southwater

Southwater is an imprint of Anness Publishing Ltd
Hermes House, 88–89 Blackfriars Road,
London SE1 8HA
tel. 020 7401 2077; fax 020 7633 9499
www.southwaterbooks.com; info@anness.com

© Anness Publishing Ltd 2004

UK agent: The Manning Partnership Ltd, 6 The Old
Dairy, Melcombe Road, Bath BA2 3LR
tel. 01225 478444; fax 01225 478440
sales@manning-partnership.co.uk

UK distributor: Grantham Book Services Ltd, Isaac
Newton Way, Alma Park Industrial Estate,
Grantham, Lincs NG31 9SD
tel. 01476 541080; fax 01476 541061
orders@gbs.tbs-ltd.co.uk

North American agent/distributor: National Book
Network, 4501 Forbes Boulevard,
Suite 200, Lanham, MD 20706
tel. 301 459 3366; fax 301 429 5746
www.nbnbooks.com

Australian agent/distributor: Pan Macmillan
Australia, Level 18, St Martins Tower
31 Market St, Sydney, NSW 2000
tel. 1300 135 113; fax 1300 135 103
customer.service@macmillan.com.au

New Zealand agent/distributor: David Bateman Ltd,
30 Tarndale Grove, Off Bush Road, Albany,
Auckland; tel. (09) 415 7664; fax (09) 415 8892

A CIP catalogue record for this book is available
from the British Library.

Publisher: Joanna Lorenz
Editorial Director: Judith Simons
Project Editor: Sarah Uttridge
Production Controller: Darren Price
Designer: Nigel Partridge

Previously published as part of a larger volume,
Gardening Through the Year

1 2 3 4 5 6 7 8 9 10

CONTENTS

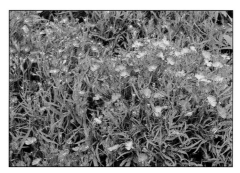

Introduction

Two of the keys to successful gardening are to carry out tasks in the right way and at the correct time. Whether it's sowing or planting, training or feeding, each needs to be carried out at a particular time according to the types of plants you are growing. The weather patterns have changed in recent years so that seasons seem less distinct than they used to be, which makes getting the timing right more difficult. This book sets out the most important gardening tasks during each season.

Planning ahead

Having all the main garden tasks mapped out through the seasons enables you to plan ahead so that you can make the most of your garden and available time. This is particularly important during the mad spring rush when it seems that everything needs to be done at once. But don't be guided by the calendar alone, since the exact timing for each task will vary from year to year depending on the prevailing weather conditions as well as the local climate and soil in your garden.

Different varieties of daffodils and tulips can be in flower from late winter through to late spring.

Rhododendrons may not have a very long season, but they are spectacular while they are in flower.

Taking action

During critical times such as early spring and autumn it's worth checking the local weather forecast each day so that you can take action if required. Simple but effective remedies, such as protecting vulnerable early sowings or newly planted tender plants from an unseasonally late frost in spring by covering them with a double layer of garden fleece or sheets of newspaper, might be all that's required to save the day. It's also worth keeping a notebook or diary of your own, so that you can fine-tune your timings in future years to best suit the conditions in your own garden.

The gardening year

As soon as the weather and soil conditions allow, you can take action to improve your border displays. Early spring is an ideal time to tackle any remodelling of existing features or creating new beds and borders from scratch. It's the perfect time for planting, and existing herbaceous perennials can be lifted and divided at this time of the year, too. If you simply want to fill gaps,

sow hardy annuals now for a cheap and cheerful display later in the year. By mid-spring, lawns will need their first cut in most areas and you should be thinking about providing support for taller perennials that are liable to flop over when in full flower later in the year. Plant tender bedding and patio containers with

Petunias, pansies and bedding geraniums (pelargoniums) will flower prolifically throughout the summer.

summer flowers as soon as the threat of frost has passed. It's also the time to improve your patio by repotting permanent container plants and making the most of any other planting pockets, cracks and crevices around paved areas.

Early summer is a time for preening and pruning to make the most of your garden plants. Removing the fading flowers from many repeat-flowering specimens will not only improve their appearance but will also help encourage further flushes of flowers later on. Many early-flowering shrubs will need to

Magnolias make a stunning seasonal focal point during spring when their waxy flowers are starkly displayed on bare branches.

be pruned to keep them within bounds and flowering well. Most hedges also need trimming as the summer progresses. On the patio, container plants will require regular watering and feeding – especially during hot, sunny spells.

By late summer, spring-flowering bulbs become available in the shops, and most of these can be planted straight away.

Autumn is another opportunity to add new plants to your garden while the soil is still warm, so that they are well established before winter sets in. All deciduous trees and shrubs can be planted, but wait until spring for evergreens, such as conifers. Winter and spring bedding can be planted as

Turn summer baskets into an autumn showcase by replanting them with winter-flowering pansies at the end of summer.

soon as the summer bedding has lost its appeal, and there's also still time to plant spring-flowering bulbs in borders, containers and naturalized in grass. Make the most of patio containers and hanging baskets, too, by planting them with winter-flowering plants as soon as the summer displays are over.

Lawns often look the worse for wear after a long, hard summer's pounding, but you can take steps in autumn to make improvements, such as sharpening edges. Ponds and other water features should be tidied up at this time of the year: removing tender aquatic plants and in colder areas protecting fish over the winter months by installing a pond heater. As the weather gets colder, not-so-hardy plants will also need protecting, either by wrapping them in some form of insulating material, or by bringing them under cover. Tender bulbs and perennials will need to be lifted and kept frost free over the winter, while container plants can be moved under cover.

Spring

The spring garden is full of hope and promise. Early bulbs, including crocuses, daffodils and hyacinths, stud beds and borders with extravagant explosions of colour all over the garden, augmented by breathtaking displays from early flowering shrubs, such as camellias, forsythia and rhododendrons. Bulbs in particular can be used to transform the overall appearance of a garden at this time of year. Whether planted in pockets around the garden, massed in containers or scattered in natural swathes across lawns or under trees they'll draw the eye and be the focus of attention. As the season progresses, colourful spring bedding such as violas, double daisies and the ever-reliable wallflower rub shoulders with serene displays of tulips and irises accompanied by popular spring-flowering shrubs, including lilacs, and magnolias. Then ornamental cherries, climbers and the first of the herbaceous plants take on the colour mantle, carrying the display seamlessly into early summer.

A spring carpet of red and yellow polyanthus, bordered by dark blue forget-me-nots, provides the perfect backdrop for the striking blooms of the 'West Point' tulip.

The Spring Garden

This is a time when gardeners need no encouragement. With lengthening days, the air less chilly, and plump buds and birdsong to stir the imagination, it is the time when gardeners cannot wait to start propagating and planting.

Early spring

Caution should be exercised in early spring, as winter seldom comes to a convenient end as spring approaches. One of the most common causes of disappointment for novice gardeners is sowing or planting too early – especially outdoors. Often, plants and seeds put out several weeks later in the season overtake ones planted earlier because they do not receive a check to growth. If you have the facilities you can make sowings indoors in pots and trays and then plant the young plants out when conditions are favourable a few weeks later. Some bedding plants, such as alyssum and French marigolds, are not worth sowing early, because they mature quickly and later sowings will flower at practically the same time as the riskier early sowings. On the other hand, a few popular plants, such as pelargoniums, need to be sown early, in a heated greenhouse or propagator, otherwise displays will be delayed or reduced. If you need only a few specimens, you may be better off buying these as young plants rather than running the risk of raising them from seed yourself.

In cold regions the weather can still be wintry at this time of the year, but in milder areas you can make a start on many outdoor jobs. If sowing or planting outdoors, bear in mind that soil temperature as well as air temperature is important. Always watch the weather forecast, and take any necessary action if frost is predicted. For example, you could cover newly planted specimens with layers of garden fleece or old newspapers at night and remove it again in the day.

Colour up the ground under deciduous trees and shrubs by planting shade-tolerant flowering plants such as this *Anemone ranunculoides*.

Combine the spring-flowering tulip 'Warbler' with early bedding like these forget-me-nots for a reliable and colourful display.

Mid-spring

For many gardeners this is the most exciting as well as the busiest time of the year. The garden looks colourful again by this time, seedlings and cuttings are growing fast, and outdoor sowing and planting can begin in earnest. This is often a time when priorities have to be decided if it isn't possible to keep up with all those urgent jobs.

Although overall temperatures may have risen, cold snaps can be even more damaging, especially if accompanied by strong winds. Not only do you still need to protect not-so-hardy plants, but new growth and flowers on hardy garden plants can also be at risk. Heavy showers are commonplace, too, which can literally wash out outdoor sowings and emerging rows of seedlings, so have a stack of cloches handy to provide temporary cover.

If you raise your own plants from seed, mid-spring is the most hectic time of the year. In the greenhouse, a wide range of seed can be sown and many popular plants can be propagated from softwood or spring cuttings too. Earlier sowings will need careful acclimatization to the harsher conditions outdoors (known as hardening off) before they can be planted out when weather conditions are suitable.

Mid-spring is also a good time to provide some support for herbaceous perennials that are prone to flopping when in full bloom. If you position supports above the growing clumps while they are still small, the plants will grow up through the supports and eventually hide them completely.

Late Spring

The end of spring can be deceptive. It often seems as though summer has already arrived, yet in cold areas there can be severe late frosts. Take local climate into account before planting any frost-tender plants outdoors. Even

A large formal border can be riotously colourful in spring, planted with blocks of tulips, wallflowers and daffodils, edged with blue polyanthus.

with experience it can be a gamble as an untypical season might produce surprises. Judging when frosts are no longer likely is mainly a matter of assessing risk. A good guide is to watch when summer bedding is put out in the local parks. These gardeners will have amassed generations of local knowledge of your area, which is by far the best guide.

Late spring is always a busy time in the gardening year. Early sowings will have been pricked out and potted on ready for hardening off and planting out in the garden. Further sowings will still need to be made, so that the pressure for greenhouse and coldframe space will be at its most intense. The weather will be improving throughout late spring so it will be safe to plant out tender plants in all except the most exposed gardens by the end of spring.

All new plants need regular care to avoid checks in growth. Young plants in pots may need to be fed with a dilute liquid feed if the weather delays planting for more than a couple of weeks. Once planted, all new additions should be kept well watered until established. Keep weeds under control, ensuring they are not allowed to flower and set seed. A mulch applied between plants will help to prevent weed seeds germinating and retain soil moisture.

Pests and diseases can be troublesome by this time, so inspect all plants regularly and take the appropriate action as soon as symptoms are noticed. Slugs and snails are the primary pest to watch out for if the weather is wet, while aphids can multiply alarmingly as temperatures rise. All can be controlled effectively by hand if you catch them early enough, although you may prefer to take preventative action, such as using barriers, chemicals or biological controls, to protect the most vulnerable plants.

Iris reticulata is a dwarf iris that loves a sunny position. Its elegant, scented flowers appear in early spring.

Sowing and planting summer flowers

Hardy annuals are among the easiest plants to grow from seed – they are undemanding of soil and can be simply sown where they are to grow. They are a cheap and easy alternative to the tender bedding plants that will be sold in garden centres later in the spring. You can either sow them in pots and seed trays for planting out around the garden as established plants, or you can sow them direct where you want them to flower.

Sowing the seed

Starting seeds off in pots or trays enables you to provide the best possible germination and growing conditions, with the seedlings safe from slugs and other pests, and you have greater control of the final

Love-in-a-mist (*Nigella*) is a wonderful airy hardy annual that is easily raised from seed sown in early spring.

effect. Sowing direct in the soil, on the other hand, means you can cover large areas easily without the cost or hassle of raising plants in pots. This works particularly well with large-seeded varieties of hardy annuals, such as pot marigold and poached egg plant. Don't be put off by the

thought of preparing a seedbed – this requires no more work than getting beds and borders ready for planting tender bedding later in the season. As long as you choose a sunny position, weed and water, and thin overcrowded seedlings, the results are almost always good. Bear in mind the final height of each variety, sowing the tallest at the back and the shortest at the front.

Sowing in rows makes thinning and weeding much easier – especially if you don't know what the seedlings look like and find it difficult to distinguish between desirable seedlings and weeds. If, however, you want to create a more natural patch of flowers, broadcast sowing (where the seed is scattered randomly) would be more appropriate. This is

SOWING HARDY ANNUALS

1 You will get best results if you prepare the ground thoroughly by digging it over and clearing it of weeds and other debris. Break up any clods and rake the surface to a fine, crumbly structure.

2 If you are growing just for cutting, sow in rows in a spare piece of ground, but if you want to make a bright border of hardy annuals, 'draw' your design on the ground with sand and grit.

3 Use the corner of a hoe or rake to draw shallow drills, but change the direction of the drills from one block to the next to avoid a regimented appearance. Check the packet for spacing between rows.

4 Sprinkle the seeds as evenly as possible. If the soil is very dry, run water into the bottom of each drill first and allow it to soak in.

5 Write and insert a label, then cover the seeds by raking the soil back over the drills. Try not to disturb the seeds unnecessarily.

6 Water thoroughly if the soil is dry. Thereafter, continue to water during dry weather until the seedlings have emerged.

PLANTING OUT SWEET PEAS

1 For general garden display and a mass of flowers, a wigwam of canes is ideal. Incline the canes inwards and tie at the top, or use a proprietary cane holder.

2 Wire or plastic netting fixed to canes to form a circular tower is another efficient way to support tall sweet peas for general garden decoration at the back of a border.

3 Excavate a hole that is large enough to accommodate the rootball with minimal disturbance, at the base of each cane, or about 23cm (9in) apart.

4 Sweet pea plants are sometimes sold with a cluster of seedlings in one pot. Always separate these and plant individually. Spread the roots out, cover, then water thoroughly.

5 Introduce the plants to their supports at an early stage. The pliable stems can be wound in and out of netting, or attached to canes with string or with metal split rings.

6 If sowing directly into the soil, sow two or three seeds at each position, and thin to one later if more germinate.

particularly useful if you have a packet of mixed annuals, for example, where you might want to create the appearance of a wild garden. After preparing the soil thoroughly, scatter the seeds as evenly as possible before raking them into the surface of the soil – first in one direction and then at right angles.

Planting or sowing sweet peas

Early spring is a good time to sow sweet peas direct outside if weather and your soil conditions allow. Sow two or three seeds at each position, and thin to one plant later if more germinate. In colder areas or on heavy soils it is not too late to sow

now indoors. Sweet pea seeds can also be sown in the autumn and overwintered in a coldframe, or sown in a greenhouse in mid- or late winter. These will now have made sturdy plants ready to be planted out. It is a good idea to try both methods, as the seedlings often succumb to slugs but they also dislike root disturbance.

Planting tender bulbs

Gladioli and most other summer-flowering bulbs, corms and tubers can be planted now, though in cold districts it is too early to plant any very frost-sensitive plants because the shoots may emerge and be killed

by a late frost. Consider growing them in rows in a spare piece of ground if you want them for cutting, but they look best planted in blocks or clusters when grown in beds and borders. As a guide to planting depth, most bulbs should be covered with twice their own depth of soil. For example, if the bulb is 2.5cm (1in) deep, cover it with 5cm (2in) of soil, though there are a few exceptions (check the packaging for details). Some tubers and corms, such as those of anemones, tend to become very dry and shrivelled after a long period in store. You can usually plump them up by soaking in water for a day before you plant.

Creating new borders

Early spring is an ideal time to make garden improvements. Simple changes, such as extending an existing border or creating a new one from scratch, can have an enormous impact on the overall design. Borders along the edge of a garden can help disguise the boundary, creating the illusion of space. Rather than having a narrow strip border along a fence, introduce gentle curves that are pleasing to look at and help lead the eye away from the edge of your plot. An island bed is another option. It has the advantage that it can be viewed from all sides, but tends to work less well if space is restricted.

Design matters

You will also need to consider the style of your garden and the type of plants you wish to grow so that they are in harmony with existing features in the overall design. Simple shapes work best in most situations, with regular circles, squares and rectangles tending to produce a more formal effect while irregular shapes enhance an informal atmosphere. The size of the border should depend on its scale when compared to other features and the overall size of the plot. It's also a good idea to bear in

You can transform the appearance and atmosphere of a garden by creating new borders or improving existing ones. Borders along the boundary can be used to help disguise unattractive fences and walls and to create the illusion of space.

CREATING A CIRCULAR BED

1 Insert a post in the centre of the proposed bed. Attach one end of a piece of string, the length of the radius, to the post and the other end to a bottle filled with sand or soil.

2 Walk slowly around the post, keeping the string taut and the bottle tilted, so the sand or soil trickles out as you walk and marks the outline of the circle.

3 View the circle from all angles to make sure that it is in proportion to the rest of the garden. Then you can remove the turf within the circle to produce a perfectly round bed.

Techniques for creating different shapes

Perfect oval Place two posts in the ground and loosely tie a piece of string around them. Experiment with the distance between the two posts and the length of the string to get the size and shape of the bed you require. Place a bottle filled with sand or soil inside the loop of string and walk around the posts, keeping the string taut. The sand or soil will trickle out, creating the outline of a perfect oval.

Kidney shape Use a flexible garden hose to work out the size and shape of an irregular or kidney-shaped bed. Then remove a line of turf around the inside edge to mark it out.

Straight lines Using a straight-edged board or plank as a guide, cut a straight edge with a spade or half-moon edging iron. Or stretch a length of garden twine between two pegs to provide a guide.

mind how much time you can spend maintaining the border. Deep borders might look dramatic, but they will be more difficult to maintain.

When you come to choosing plants, make sure they are suitable for the site and soil. Space them to accommodate their ultimate height and spread, positioning the largest at the back (the centre of an island bed) and progressively smaller growing varieties towards the edge. Choose plants with an upright habit for the back of a boundary border so that they provide sufficient cover without taking up too much ground space. In a mixed border, choose shrubs to form the backbone of the border that are interesting in their own right and will provide a useful foil for other plants. Fill the gaps with perennials, bulbs and groundcover plants. Try to use a mixture of evergreen and deciduous plants so that the display looks good and ever-changing throughout the year.

Preparing the ground

Because flowerbeds and borders are likely to be left undisturbed for many years it is important to clear the area of weeds completely and prepare the soil well. If it is cut into a lawn, you should skim off the turf with a spade. Elsewhere, you can dig out the weeds by hand, spray with a suitable herbicide or cover the area with black plastic sheeting for several months to kill the weeds. Dig the soil thoroughly and incorporate well-rotted organic matter. Digging is best carried out in late autumn on heavy soils, so that the large clods can be exposed to the weathering effects of frost. Dig the first trench to one spade's depth across the plot, and transfer the soil you have removed in a wheelbarrow to the other end of the plot, where it will be used to fill the final trench. Fork a layer of well-rotted compost or manure into the bottom of the trench to improve the soil structure and to provide nutrients for the plants. Dig the next trench across the plot, turning the soil on to the compost in the first trench. Add compost to the new trench and then dig the next.

Continue down the border until the whole of the surface has been turned. Add compost to the final trench and then fill it with the soil from the first trench. Allow the soil to settle and then rake level, removing any new weeds or other debris that come to the surface.

In a formal garden, straight borders can be used to reinforce the overall appearance. Here, standard roses have been underplanted by spring-flowering bulbs to extend the period of interest.

Dividing and planting perennials

If they are left undisturbed, most perennials eventually become congested at the roots, which reduces vigour and flowering. You can improve your displays by lifting and dividing overgrown clumps every few years. Not only will you get bigger and better flowers, but the plants will remain healthier and you will also get hundreds of free plants that you can use elsewhere in the garden, sell for charity or give away. Regular lifting and dividing also enables you to clear established borders of troublesome perennial weeds, such as couch grass.

Dividing perennials

Perennials can be divided in spring or autumn, but spring is best for plants of borderline hardiness as well as for those perennials that flower late in the season. Some perennials, such as astilbe, liriope and solidago, respond to frequent division. Others, such as agapanthus, alstroemeria, eryngium and hellebores, do not like being disturbed and can take several

Anemone ranunculoides 'Pleniflora' will spread, forming a carpet of cheerful yellow flowers each spring.

SIMPLE DIVISION

1 The day before you plan to divide it, water the plant thoroughly. Dig up a clump of the plant, in this case Michaelmas daisy (*Aster novi-belgii*).

3 You can replant a few of the most vigorous pieces in the bed, but dig over the soil first, removing any weeds and adding some well-rotted organic material.

2 Insert two forks back to back into the plant and lever apart by gently pushing the handles to and fro. Keep on dividing the rootball until the pieces are of the desired size. Discard any exhausted, woody sections.

4 Alternatively, small pieces of the plant can be potted up individually. After watering, place these in a closed coldframe until well established, then plant out after hardening off.

years to recover from the process. Perennials that have not been divided for a long time tend to produce all their most vigorous shoots towards the edge of the clump, with weaker growth in the older, central portion.

How you divide a perennial will depend on the type of roots it produces and how long it has been since it was last divided. For most perennials you should be able to ease the crown apart using two border forks held back to back and pushed and pulled against each other. Looser rootballs can be teased apart by hand, while a few might need slicing into sections using an old kitchen knife. Really tough, woody clumps are more easily sliced into sections with a sharp spade. No matter what

method you use, lift the clump out of the border and into an open space such as on a lawn, path or patio, so that you can move around it easily without damaging other plants. If the clump is very large, slice it into sections that are small enough to carry out of the border. Discard the least vigorous central sections of each clump and replant only healthy divisions, each with plenty of shoots and roots, that are free of perennial weed roots. Clear the border of weeds and improve the soil by adding well-rotted organic matter and a handful of slow-release fertilizer before replanting. Water well after planting and keep well watered during dry spells throughout summer and autumn.

Planting herbaceous borders

Herbaceous border plants can be planted at any time from containers, but most gardeners prefer to get them planted in spring so that they contribute to the summer show. If you buy plants by mail order they may arrive as small root-wrapped plants, and these should be planted before the new shoots emerge or while they are still very short.

If your herbaceous plants are root-wrapped, keep them in a cool, shady place until you are ready to plant. Make sure that the plants are kept moist at all times. Remove the wrapping only just before you are ready to plant. Spread out the roots widely within the planting hole before

You can create a striking effect in a large, informal herbaceous border by restricting the colour scheme to just two colours. Red and yellow look particularly good in bright sunshine.

PLANTING HERBACEOUS PLANTS

1 If planting a border, lay the plants out first so that you can visualize the result, spacing them to allow for growth. Adjust them until you are satisfied with the arrangement.

2 Water the plants about an hour before you start and knock them out of their pots only when you are ready to plant. Tease out any roots that circle the rootball before planting.

3 Make sure that the ground is clear of weeds before planting, and work methodically from the back of the border or from one end. You will be able to plant most herbaceous perennials with a trowel or hand fork, but you may need a spade for large plants.

4 Return the soil, making sure that the plant is at its original depth, and firm well to eliminate any pockets of air around the roots, which could cause them to dry out. Water well both after planting and during any dry spells until established.

returning the soil. Root-wrapped plants are more vulnerable than container-grown plants until they become established, so take extra care and keep them well watered.

Planting container plants

Container-grown perennials can be planted at any time of the year provided the soil is not too wet or frozen. However, planting in early spring allows you to enjoy their flowering display in their first year. Water the plants before planting. Prepare the ground thoroughly, removing weeds and any other debris. Perennial weeds should be removed complete with their roots. Make a hole for each plant and set them at the same level as they were in the pot. Firm the soil around each plant and level the soil after planting, before watering well. Mulch around new plants with a loose organic material, such as well-rotted garden compost or manure, to help reduce water loss and prevent competition from weeds.

Planting trees and shrubs

Spring is an ideal time to plant shrubs and trees because the soil is moist and is beginning to warm up so that new root growth will help the plant become established quickly. You can plant container-grown specimens any time provided the ground is not too wet or frozen. You can plant bare-rooted specimens during winter or early spring.

Planting distance

An important consideration when planting shrubs and trees is the distance that should be left between them. A common error is to place new specimens far too close together, so that within a few years the difficult decision of which to remove has to be made. You can avoid unbalancing the overall design in this way by checking how big the shrubs are likely to grow in a good gardening encyclopedia and then calculating your plant spacing to accommodate them. You may find that initially the newly planted border can appear rather stark, especially if you have bought small specimens. However, this can be overcome by filling the gaps in the early years with a scattering of hardy annuals, short-lived perennials or groundcover plants that can be removed as the shrubs and trees take up more space.

If you want to achieve instant results, choose a range of quick-growing shrubs, such as butterfly bush (*Buddleja*), lavatera, sambucus and ceanothus, mixed with a selection of specimen evergreens and groundcover plants. If they are watered and fed well, the border should fill out in just a couple of years.

Preparing the site

The most important task is to prepare the planting site thoroughly by removing perennial weed roots and incorporating well-rotted manure or garden compost. Always plant the specimen at the same depth as it was in the pot and water well before planting. Dig a hole slightly larger than the pot or rootball and then check the depth by placing the specimen in the hole and laying a cane across it. Add or take away soil as necessary, then position the specimen again. Bare-rooted trees should be inspected for damaged roots, which should be trimmed using a pair of secateurs (pruners). Check the rootball of container-grown shrubs and trees and unwind any roots circling the base of the rootball.

Staking trees

Taller trees will need staking to keep them upright and help them to establish quickly. All trees in an exposed garden should be staked at planting time, with the stake put on the windward side. Bare-rooted trees can be secured using a short vertical stake hammered into the hole at this stage. Container-grown trees are best staked after planting using an angled stake that does not interfere with the rootball. Attach the tree to the stake using an adjustable tree tie, which can be loosened as the tree grows, so that its stem is not constricted as it expands.

To make sure there are no air pockets around the roots, trickle a little soil around the roots, shake the plant gently and add more soil. Firm lightly as you go. Use your heel to firm the soil around all trees and shrubs after planting and water well. Cover the surface with a mulch to keep down weed germination and help prevent the soil from drying out. Organic mulches will slowly become incorporated into the soil by worms and other soil-borne organisms, improving its texture and providing nutrients, so top them up each spring to maintain their effectiveness.

Quick-growing shrubs, such as this semi-evergreen lavatera, are ideal for filling gaps in borders, helping a new garden to appear lush and well-established.

PLANTING A SHRUB

1 Always clear the area of weeds, especially any deep-rooted perennials, which will be difficult to eradicate if they grow within the root system of the shrub. Dig in plenty of garden compost or rotted manure.

2 Water the plant well an hour before planting. Dig a hole about twice the width of the pot or rootball. Position the plant and place a stick across the hole to make sure it will be at its original depth.

3 Remove the shrub from its container, taking care not to damage the roots. If roots are wound tightly around the inside of the pot, tease some of them out to encourage them to grow out into the surrounding soil.

4 Place the rootball in the hole. Holding the plant upright, fill the hole around the rootball and firm the soil down well to eliminate any air pockets.

5 To get your shrub off to a good start, apply a general garden fertilizer at the recommended rate around the plant. Keep away from the stem. Water well.

6 'Balled' or 'root-wrapped' shrubs are sold with their roots wrapped in hessian, a plastic or metal cage or some other material. Check the depth of the planting hole as before.

7 When the plant is in position, untie the wrapping and slide it into the hole. Avoid disturbing the ball of soil around the roots.

8 Replace the soil, and firm well to eliminate pockets of air. Apply fertilizer and water as described for container-grown plants.

9 It is worth mulching the ground after planting to conserve moisture and suppress weeds, which will compete for nutrients.

Pruning trees and shrubs

Most trees and shrubs do not need regular pruning, other than to remove dead, damaged or diseased material. If space is restricted, however, you may have to prune annually to keep them within bounds. A few trees and shrubs will produce better displays if they are cut back at the right time and in the right way. How you prune will depend largely on the plant you are dealing with and the type of growth you are trying to promote.

Pruning strategies

If you are pruning to improve flowering you will need to know whether the shrub blooms on wood produced during the previous season or on new wood produced during the current season. However, if you do not know anything about the shrub you could use the fail-safe one-in-three method. Prune one-third of the shrub back each year, choosing the oldest stems – so after three years, no stem is more than three years old. The one-in-three method is also a good way of rejuvenating old shrubs, such as you might find in a neglected garden filled with overgrown, unfamiliar plants.

Many popular shrubs can be improved by regular pruning in early spring. Only prune shrubs that you

Pruning *Spiraea japonica* 'Goldflame' during early spring will produce more compact shrubs with brighter and bigger foliage.

know require spring pruning, otherwise you may cut out the shoots that will bear this year's flowers. If in doubt, consult an encyclopedia that gives pruning information. You can get improved flowering from quick-growing shrubs that flower on the current season's growth, such as *Buddleja davidii*, *Hydrangea paniculata* and lavatera, by pruning them before new growth starts. Similarly, shrubs such as dogwood (*Cornus*) and *Spiraea japonica* 'Goldflame', that are mainly grown for their decorative stems and colourful foliage, can be pruned now to enhance the display the following

winter. Another example, the whitewash bramble (*Rubus cockburnianus*), is cut back to the ground annually in early spring because of the appeal of the white bloom on the new growth. New shoots will soon grow and the plant will be just as attractive next winter. Indeed, the colour on young stems is more pronounced and the plant is more attractive if all the canes have been produced in the current year.

On the other hand, grey-leaved plants (such as lavenders, *Santolina chamaecyparissus* and senecio) can be pruned lightly in early spring to keep them compact and the foliage dense. Do not cut back into old wood because this is unlikely to re-shoot.

Deadheading heathers

The removal of fading flowers, known as deadheading, is a quick and easy technique that will help keep heathers looking neat. In early spring, trim them with shears. Cut just below faded flowers but avoid cutting into the old wood because it will not re-shoot.

PRUNING WHITEWASH BRAMBLES

1 Cut old canes of *Rubus cockburnianus* to just above the ground using secateurs (pruners). New shoots will appear from below ground.

2 You might find it easier to use long-handled pruners (loppers) to cut back the oldest and thickest stems, which will be tough and woody.

SPRING PRUNING SHRUBS

1 Prune shrubs grown for coloured winter stems shortly before new growth starts. These include *Cornus alba* and *Cornus stolonifera* cultivars and *Salix alba* subsp. *vitellina* 'Britzensis'. Only prune plants that have been established for a few years.

2 Cut back all the stems to an outward-facing bud about 5cm (2in) from the ground or from the stump of old, hard wood.

3 Although the pruning seems drastic, new, more vigorous and brightly coloured shoots will soon appear and by next winter will make a splendid sight. Prune annually if you feed and mulch the plants, otherwise prune back established plants every second spring.

4 Trim over grey-leaved shrubs, such as the popular *Santolina chamaecyparissus* and *Helichrysum angustifolium*, to keep them neat and compact. Take care not to cut into old, woody stems, which will not re-shoot.

5 If you prune the plant regularly from a young age, prune back close to the base to a point where you can see new shoots developing. This may be as low as 10cm (4in) from the ground on some plants.

6 The plant will look bare and sparse after pruning, but within a month should be well clothed again. Lightly fork in some slow-release fertilizer around the shrub to encourage new stems.

7 *Buddleja davidii* produces its flowers at the tops of tall, lanky stems if left unpruned. Each spring, cut back all the shoots to within about two buds of the previous year's growth.

8 Again, this type of pruning looks drastic but it will greatly enhance the look of the plant later in the year by encouraging vigorous, productive stems.

Pollarding

Pollarded shrubs and trees are grown on a short trunk with their main stems pruned back to a framework each spring. The previous season's growth is almost completely removed in early spring by pruning back to within 5cm (2in) of the established framework, leaving one or two buds on each stem to regrow. *Eucalyptus gunnii*, *Sambucus nigra* and cotinus all benefit from this sort of treatment and will produce more colourful leaves.

Pruning roses and climbers

Roses and clematis have both developed an undeserved reputation for being difficult to prune. Until fairly recently rose enthusiasts would have you believe that the only way to get a decent display from your bushes was to follow an intensive care programme of pruning, feeding and disease control. Recent research, however, has shown that rose pruning needn't be an exact science and that it can be done quickly and easily by anyone.

Pruning roses

Trials have shown that you can achieve very good results from hybrid tea (large-flowered) and floribunda (cluster-flowered) roses simply by cutting them roughly to an even height with secateurs or even a hedgetrimmer without worrying about the detailed pruning. The conventional method is still practised by most rose enthusiasts, however. Don't worry if you make one or two wrong cuts – the roses will probably still bloom prolifically. Given a moist, fertile soil, regularly enriched with organic material, roses should grow strongly enough to withstand most pest and disease attacks.

To get the most from your climbing rose, such as this deliciously scented, double pink 'Madame Grégoire Staechelin', prune it in early spring so that you can enjoy a bumper crop of delightful early-summer flowers followed by large, round, bright red hips in autumn.

PRUNING BUSH AND SHRUB ROSES

1 Moderate pruning is the most appropriate for established hybrid tea roses. Cut back the stems by about half, to an outward-facing bud to keep the centre of the bush open.

2 You can treat floribundas in the same way, but if you prune the oldest shoots severely and others lightly, flowering may be spread over a longer period.

3 Whichever type of rose you are pruning, cut back any dead, damaged or diseased shoots to healthy wood, making a clean, slanting cut.

Roses do need to be pruned regularly, however. This is because rose stems will continue to grow and flower well only for a few years before they become exhausted. You can reinvigorate the plant by pruning back exhausted stems to a healthy bud lower down that will grow into a vigorous, free-flowering new shoot. In nature old stems wither and die back, allowing newer stems to take over. By pruning you are simply speeding up this recycling process and you'll also help to keep the shrub compact and healthy. Early spring is the ideal time to prune all bush and shrub roses, including miniatures.

Pruning clematis

The mystique surrounding clematis pruning has probably developed because they are not all pruned in the same way. However, as long as you know when your clematis flowers and whether it flowers on the current season's growth or stems produced during the previous season, you won't go far wrong. Clematis are divided into three groups: early-flowering forms that produce blooms on last year's stems only (known as Group 1); those that flower during late spring and early summer on last year's stems and again during late summer on growth produced in the current season (known as Group 2); and those that flower during late

Pruning standard roses

It's essential to maintain an even shape to the head of a standard rose. Prune ordinary standard roses now using secateurs (pruners), cutting out broken or damaged stems and then reducing the remaining stems by about two-thirds. Weeping standards should be pruned like ramblers in autumn.

PRUNING A CLIMBING ROSE

Repeat-flowering climbing roses that bear blooms in a series of flushes throughout the summer can be pruned in early spring. Remove any weak and old stems entirely. Also, cut back stems that flowered during the previous year by one-third to a half and trim any sideshoots on the remaining stems to two or three buds. Tie in the pruned stems using soft string or plant ties.

summer only on new growth (known as Group 3). All types of clematis can be pruned in early spring if necessary.
- **Group 1** Spring-flowering clematis, such as cultivars of *C. alpina*, *C. armandii*, *C. cirrhosa*, *C. macropetala* and *C. montana*, need pruning only when they have to be restrained. Cut out sufficient branches to reduce congestion and cut those that encroach beyond their space back to their point of origin or to a pair of plump buds.
- **Group 2** Includes late-spring-flowering and early summer varieties, such as 'Barbara Jackman', 'Daniel Deronda', 'Lasurstern', 'Marie Boisselot', 'Nelly Moser', 'Richard Pennell', 'The President' and 'Vyvyan Pennell'. After cutting out

all the dead, damaged or weak growth, remove any wood that is making the clematis congested, cutting back to a pair of strong buds. Leave strong, healthy stems unpruned, or trim back only lightly (these will carry the first flush of flowers).
- **Group 3** Includes late-summer-flowering clematis, such as 'Bill Mackenzie', 'Ernest Markham', 'Etiole Violette', 'Jackmanii', 'Perle d'Azur' and 'Ville de Lyon'. These are perhaps the easiest of all to prune since all stems should be cut back during early spring to the lowest pair of plump buds.

Pruning honeysuckles

These popular climbers either flower on the current season's growth or on stems produced during the previous season. Honeysuckles that flower on new shoots do not need regular pruning unless they get out of hand. Forms that flower on the previous year's growth should have stems that have flowered cut back to a newer shoot lower down on the stem.

RENOVATING A HONEYSUCKLE

Prune honeysuckles only if the flowers are too high or the growth too thick and tangled. If you don't know the variety, cut the oldest stems that have flowered the previous season back to a newer shoot lower down.

Lawn improvements

If you have a patchy area of grass that needs improving, you can either oversow it with grass seed or create a new lawn from scratch. If you want to oversow an existing lawn, rake the area thoroughly to remove thatch (the dead moss and grass that collects at the base of the grass blades in the lawn), prick over any bare areas with a fork and sow seed at half the rate per square metre/yard you would for a new lawn. Rake the seed into the bare patches, water well and use black cotton to protect the area from birds.

Making a new lawn

Before you create a new lawn, you will have to decide whether to raise it from seed or to lay turf. The main advantages of a lawn from seed are that it is cheaper and easier than laying turf and you can choose from a range of grass seed mixtures, including formulations for hot or shady and dry sites. You can even get specially hard-wearing grass mixtures for a family lawn. Some turf specialists also offer seed mixtures to suit your specific requirements, but these can be expensive. Even ordinary turf may cost four times as much per square metre/yard as seed, and it is the less flexible option because it has to be laid as soon as it arrives, no matter what the weather or soil conditions. Turfing large areas is also hard work, but turf gives near instant results, whereas a lawn grown from seed can take up to six months before it's usable.

Whichever method you choose it is important that you prepare the ground thoroughly if you want to achieve a quality lawn. You will need to begin work several weeks before sowing or planned delivery of the

PREPARING THE GROUND

1 Dig the ground thoroughly, and make every effort to eliminate difficult or deep-rooted perennial weeds. Then rake the soil level. Use a system of pegs, levelled with a spirit level on a straight-edge, to set the height.

2 Allow the soil to settle for a week, then consolidate it further by treading it evenly to remove large air pockets. If you do not have a roller, the best way to do this is to shuffle your feet over the area, first in one direction, then in the other.

3 Rake the consolidated soil to produce a fine crumbly structure suitable for sowing seeds. If you can, leave the area for a couple of weeks to allow weed seeds to germinate. Hoe them off or use a weedkiller that leaves the ground safe for replanting within days.

LAWNS FROM SEED

1 Choose a windless day and sow grass seed as evenly as possible. You will get better results by being more systematic about your approach. Use string and canes to divide the area into 1m (1yd) strips, and divide these into 1m (1yd) squares.

2 Use a small container that holds enough seed for a square metre/yard (make a mark on it if the amount only partly fills the container). Scatter the seeds as evenly as possible with a sweeping motion of the hand, first in one direction and then at right angles.

3 If you have to sow a large area it might be worth hiring a seed/fertilizer distributor that you can simply wheel over the area. Always check the delivery rate over sheets of paper or plastic first. Lightly rake the seed into the surface. Water if necessary to keep the soil moist.

You can improve the appearance of established lawns by oversowing threadbare patches at this time of the year. Use a suitable seed mixture to match the existing lawn.

seed should germinate about a week after sowing if the soil and weather conditions are favourable. Wait until the grass blades are 8cm (3in) long before making your first cut, setting the blade height to trim just the tips. This will encourage the grass seedlings to shoot from the base and create a thicker lawn more quickly. Thereafter, reduce the cutting height and trim when the grass gets to 5–8cm (2–3in) for the first season. It is essential that you keep the mower blade sharp so that the seedlings are not ripped out of the ground as you mow. Wait until next spring before you feed your lawn with a spring feed.

If you don't have time to prepare the ground properly this spring, delay sowing seed or laying turf until the autumn instead.

turf. On heavy soils it is often easier to prepare the site in autumn, ready for a new lawn in spring. Choose a fine day when the soil is workable and clear it of all existing grass, perennial weeds and other debris. Dig the area thoroughly and leave large clods to be broken down by frost action over the winter. In early spring, rake the area level and remove any debris that has worked its way to the surface. Mark out the site with pegs and use a spirit level to check the level. Once the site is level, firm it by treading – using tiny shuffling steps with the weight on your heels. Repeat this process until you have created a firm, level bed. Finally, rake the soil carefully from different directions to produce an even surface with a fine breadcrumb-like texture – perfect for both sowing and laying turf (see left and right).

Keep your new lawn well watered until it is established. Turves must receive sufficient water to dampen the soil beneath or the roots will not grow down into the ground. Grass

LAWNS FROM TURF

1 Use a plank to stand on while you lay the next row, since this will help to avoid damaging the turf you have just laid. Stagger the joints between rows to create a bond like brickwork. Make sure these do not align.

2 Tamp down each row of turf (you can use the head of a rake as shown), then move the plank forwards to lay the next row. The turf will be firmed by your weight as you work off the plank laying subsequent rows.

3 Brush sieved sandy soil, or a mixture of peat and sand, into the joints. This will help to bind the turves together.

4 Shape edges when the lawn is laid. Lay a hose as a guide for a curved edge, or use a plank of wood for a straight edge.

Using flower supports

There are few things more disappointing than seeing herbaceous borders collapse just as they're coming into flower. Blustery winds, heavy rain or just the sheer weight of the developing flowerheads can be to blame. It is, therefore, worthwhile taking steps to support vulnerable plants before they topple. Fortunately, not all herbaceous plants require staking (see below for varieties that usually do not), but those that do should be tackled now before they have put on too much growth. Always keep a supply of canes and string in reserve for emergency repairs after a storm.

Methods of support

First of all, you can reduce the need for plant supports by growing the right plants in the right place and encouraging them to produce strong,

Most delphiniums, except the dwarf varieties, need staking to ensure they do not fall over. It is well worth the effort when they produce their beautiful tall spikes of flowers. They come in many colours – this white variety is 'Sandpiper'.

Well-behaved perennials

Acanthus	Hosta
Agapanthus	Iris
Alchemilla	Kniphofia
Alstroemeria	Liatris
Anchusa	Limonium
Anemone ×	Liriope
hybrida	Lychnis
Astilbe	Lysimachia
Begonia	Lythrum
Brunnera	Nepeta
Centaurea	Oenothera
Crocosmia	Penstemon
Dianthus	Polemonium
Dicentra	Potentilla
Dictamnus	erecta
Digitalis	Pulmonaria
Echinops	Salvia
Euphorbia	Scabiosa
Filipendula	Schizostylus
Gaillardia	Sedum
Geranium	Senecio
Geum	Stachys
Helleborus	Trollius
Hemerocallis	Verbascum
Heuchera	Veronica

self-supporting growth. Most herbaceous plants (unless of course they are shade-loving varieties) should be grown in a sunny, well-drained spot. If grown in the shade they will become drawn and weak, so will be much more likely to collapse. For this reason, herbaceous plants grown in a border next to a fence are less able to support themselves than the same plants grown in an island bed where they get much more light from all sides. Giving a high-potash fertilizer without a lot of nitrogen will also encourage smaller, sturdier plants which will need less staking.

There are several types of support you can use. The style you choose will depend on the type of plants you are growing and your attitude to gardening. If you are well organized and do not mind the sight of wiry supports in your borders, you can position hoops, stakes and canes early in the season before the plants have had time to grow. If, however, you have a just-in-time approach to

gardening or prefer to keep your garden free of wiry clutter you may prefer to opt for supports that can be carefully positioned much later in the season. In an informal garden or a prominent border traditional twiggy sticks are the least obtrusive supports. If they are carefully entwined, they can bring a rustic charm to borders as well as acting as an effective support when the plants grow up through them. You can buy such material from garden centres in early spring, but the cheapest option is to recycle twiggy prunings from hedges and shrubs. Bamboo canes and string are the next cheapest option but are time-consuming to erect if you've got a lot of plants to support. You can also buy purpose-made wire hoops and linking stakes, which are easy to use and very effective.

Choosing your support

Which type of support you choose should also depend on the type of

STAKING BORDER PLANTS

1 Proprietary hoops with adjustable legs can be placed over a clump-forming perennial. The new shoots grow through the grid, gaining support from the frame and eventually hiding it.

2 Tall flowering stems can be staked individually by tying them to a cane that is shorter than the eventual height of the plant and hidden from sight behind the stem.

3 Wire netting can be used vertically, creating cylinders, held firmly in place with posts. The plant grows up through the centre, with the leaves coming through and covering the sides.

plant you are supporting. Those that produce sprawling growth could be supported with unobtrusive twiggy sticks, while those that form multi-stemmed clumps would be best supported using proprietary wire stakes or a circle of bamboo canes linked with string. If you are growing a whole border of such plants, you could save a lot of time by using large-mesh plastic netting. If it is supported on large stakes either end of the bed, it can be held taut over the plants and gradually raised as they grow. Herbaceous plants that produce large flowerspikes, such as delphiniums, gladioli and hollyhocks, are generally best supported individually, using a single bamboo cane and split-ring ties. Stakes should be pushed 15–30cm (6–12in) into the ground.

Stay safe

Eye injuries caused by the sharp ends of supporting stakes when weeding and working around herbaceous plants are among the most common injuries in the garden. The best way to avoid such problems is to carry

out any maintenance work before staking and use supports that are easily seen. Very short supports (less than your arm's length) and taller supports (a lot longer than your arm's length) are far less likely to cause injuries, so bear this in mind

when you choose supports for your plants. Clearly marking the ends of canes using decorative cane tops or colourful ends that can be easily seen is another option. An alternative way of protecting your eyes is to wear a pair of protective goggles.

Lupins do not always need support, especially in a sheltered position, but it is usually safer to stake the tall varieties. They should quickly grow up to hide the stakes.

Looking after your lawn

Caring for your lawn will begin to take up a lot of your gardening time from now onwards. Obviously, the larger your lawn the more time it will take to maintain to keep it looking at its best. However, you can cut down on the maintenance time by making some simple changes to the shape, by choosing the right size mower for your lawn and by installing a mowing strip (see below).

Cutting the workload

You will be more efficient if you choose an appropriately sized mower for the area you have to cut. For example, if you have a small lawn – say less than 50 square metres (60 square yards) – a mower with a cutting width of around 25cm (10in) should be sufficient, but for large lawns – over 250 square metres (300 square yards) – you'd be better off with a self-propelled mower with a cutting width of at least 35cm (14in). Consider a ride-on model for lawns that are much larger than this.

A lush green lawn is an essential element of most gardens, and a simple shape with straight edges and no obstacles in the middle makes mowing an easy task.

The overall shape of your lawn will also influence how difficult and time-consuming it is to cut. Irregular shapes have a longer perimeter, so there is more length of edge to cut and it is necessary to keep stopping to turn the mower more often. Obstacles such as island beds, children's play equipment and ponds will also slow you down. This

CREATING A MOWING EDGE

1 A mowing edge of bricks or paving slabs will prevent overhanging flowers smothering the edge of the lawn and make it easier to mow. Mark out the area of grass to be lifted, using the paving as a guide. To keep the new edge straight, use a half-moon edger against the paving. Then lift the grass to be removed by slicing it off with a spade.

2 Remove enough soil along the edge of the lawn to allow for the depth of the slab and foundation. Make a firm base by compacting gravel or a mixture of sand and gravel where the paving is to be laid. Use a plank of wood to make sure it is level, removing and adding soil as necessary. Allow for the thickness of the paving and a few blobs of mortar.

3 It is best to bed the edging on mortar to give stability, but because it will not be taking a heavy weight, there is no need for a whole bed of mortar. Press the slabs on to blobs of mortar and tap them level with a mallet. The slabs should be laid evenly and be flush with, or very slightly below, the lawn. Use a spirit level to double check.

SOWING WILDFLOWERS

1 The most satisfactory way to create a wildflower meadow is to sow a special mixture of wildflower seeds. Clear the ground completely of all perennial weeds before you start. Don't add fertilizer to the soil since wildflowers do best in impoverished conditions.

2 Sow the seeds evenly and then rake them in, first in one direction and then the other. It does not matter if some seeds remain on the surface. Keep them well watered until the seeds germinate. Protect from birds with black cotton or twigs if necessary.

3 For a very small area, wildflower plants may be more convenient. You can raise your own from seed or buy them as tiny plug plants or larger specimens. Plant them into bare ground or in an existing lawn. Keep the plants well watered until they are established.

may not seem significant each time you mow, but when it is added up over a whole season you could be wasting a whole day of gardening time. Perhaps the least loved of all lawn maintenance tasks is trimming the edges. This can be avoided altogether by installing a mowing strip at the start of the season. You'll also never have to re-cut the edge of your lawn, which is often an annual task on light, sandy soils.

Creating a meadow

If you have a very large lawn and want to minimize maintenance leave part of it to grow longer to form a meadow. Keep the grass nearest the house neatly trimmed, with the end of the lawn merging into the wildflower meadow at the end of the plot. The easiest way to create a wildflower meadow is to sow it from scratch using a special seed mixture, but you can convert an existing lawn by clearing patches and sowing these or by planting pot-grown wildflowers direct into the grass (see above). In shady areas try primroses and wild orchids, and add bluebells,

snakeshead fritillary, snowdrops and wood anemones; in sun plant bird's-foot trefoil, corn marigold, mayweed, oxeye daisy, field poppy, speedwell and sweet violets. Wildflower areas require cutting just twice a year – once in early spring and the second time in mid- to late summer – but areas that include spring-flowering bulbs should be left until six weeks after the bulbs have finished flowering. Hire or buy a powered scythe for the job. If you want to mix bulbs with wildflowers, plant the bulbs in drifts at the perimeter of the area, so that they can be left undisturbed until the bulb foliage starts to turn yellow.

Mowing edges

Mid-spring is an ideal time to install an edge to your lawn alongside beds and borders. Traditional lawn edging strips, made from wood, metal or plastic, are ideal for keeping the edge sharp and neat. This is particularly important for lawns on light, sandy soils because the edges are easily damaged and would otherwise need re-cutting every year. If you have a

lot of overhanging plants or want to cut down on the time it takes to maintain your lawn, a mowing strip would be a better option. It is simply a paved edge that runs along the perimeter of the lawn. It can be wide enough to form a path or as narrow as a single brick if space is restricted. Set the paved edge into the ground so that it is flush with the lawn – then you can run over it with the lawnmower, eliminating the need for trimming the edge afterwards.

A mowing edge will lessen your work on a lawn, as the mower can get right over the edge of the lawn. You may have to trim any spreading grass stems, but this will only be necessary occasionally.

Making a new pond

To look good a pond needs to be positioned in a natural-looking setting within the garden. Ideally, it should be sited in full sun, well away from overhanging trees. A nearby tree, even if not close enough to create heavy shade, can cause problems by dropping leaves into the pond. Although it will look natural if it is at the lowest point in a garden, this is not necessarily the best place. Experiment with a garden hose in several positions before you start to dig. The size and shape will depend on personal taste, but it should reflect the overall design of the garden. Check there are no hidden underground obstructions, such as pipes and cables, before you excavate the hole.

Practical matters

To be self-sustaining, make your pond as big as possible, with a surface area of at least 5 square metres (over 50 square feet). Make the deepest areas at least 60cm (24in) so that the water does not get too warm in summer. Smaller ponds will also require more maintenance, clearing overgrown plants and topping up the water level during hot spells. If you want to grow marginal plants, the pond will need a shallow shelf along at least one edge about 23cm (9in) below the surface. Make the shelf at least 23cm (9in) wide so that there is plenty of room for the plants.

There are various ways to line a pond. Concrete is very durable, but requires more skill and expertise than using bought pond liners. In most circumstances it is easiest to construct a pond using either a pre-formed rigid shell or a flexible liner. The main advantage of a rigid pond liner is that you don't have to worry about designing the shape. They are available in both formal and informal designs in a range of

INSTALLING A FLEXIBLE LINER

1 Mark out the pond shape. Use garden hose or rope for an irregular shape and pegs and string for straight edges. Remove any turf and start to excavate the pond. Redistribute topsoil to other parts of the garden.

2 Dig the whole area to about 23cm (9in) deep, then mark the positions of the marginal shelves to about 23cm (9in) wide. Dig deeper areas to at least 60cm (24in) deep. Angle all vertical sides so they slope slightly inwards.

3 Check the levels as you work. Correct discrepancies using sieved garden soil. Make sure there are no sharp stones on the base and sides that might damage the liner, then line the hole with builders' sand.

4 On stony soil you may need to line the hole further with loft insulation, old carpet or a special pond liner underlay (which is expensive). Trim the liner underlay so that it fits neatly into the hole.

5 Ease the liner into position without stretching it unduly. Choose a warm day, as it will be more flexible. Weigh down the edges with stones, then fill the pond slowly with water. Ease the liner into position so that it follows the contours as the pool fills.

6 Once the pond is full, trim back the excess liner to leave an overlap of at least 15cm (6in) around the edge. Cover the overlapping liner with paving or other edging. To disguise the liner, overlap the edging at the water's edge by 2.5cm (1in).

MAKING A POND USING A RIGID LINER

1 Place the pre-formed unit on the ground and transfer the shape to the ground by inserting canes around the edge of the unit. Use a garden hose, rope or sand to mark the outline on the ground.

2 Remove the unit and canes and excavate the hole to approximately the depth of the unit plus at least 5cm (2in), following the profile of the shelves as accurately as possible.

3 Use a spirit level and straight-edged board, laid across the rim, to check that the hole is level. Measure down from the board to check that it is the required depth.

4 Remove any large stones and pad a layer of fine soil or sand in the bottom of the hole. Put the pond in the hole, then add or remove soil to ensure a snug and level fit. Check with a spirit level that the pond is level.

5 Remove the pond and line the hole with damp sand if the soil is stony. With the pond in position and the levels checked again, backfill with sand or fine soil, being careful not to push the pond out of level.

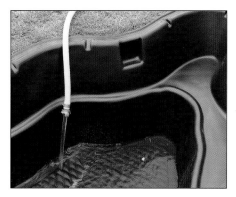

6 Fill with fresh water and backfill further if necessary as the water level rises, checking the level frequently to make sure the unit has not moved. Allow to stand for a few days before stocking with plants.

sizes. However, they do not come in very large sizes, and they tend to be more difficult to install than flexible liners. If you want to create an unusual shaped pond you'll have to choose a flexible liner, but it can be difficult to get the shape that you want on very light soils. Rigid liners are made from either fibreglass or plastic, while flexible liners are available in PVC, butyl rubber, LDPE or polythene. The latter is the cheapest but will only last for a few years before it will need to be replaced. To calculate the size of flexible liner use this formula:

• Length = 2 × maximum depth + maximum length of the pond.

• Width = 2 × maximum depth + maximum width of the pond.

For example, for a pond that is 3 × 2m (10 × 6ft) with a maximum depth of 50cm (20in), you will need a flexible liner that is 4 × 3m (14 × 10ft).

Edging your pond

The material you choose to edge your pond should reflect the formality of the pond. The clean straight lines of paving slabs are an ideal choice for formal ponds. Lay the slabs on top of the edge of the liner so that there is at least 15cm (6in) of liner under the edging stones. The edging stones should

overhang the surface of the pond by 2.5cm (1in) and be clear of the pond's water level. Make sure they are well-secured on a bed of mortar. For more informal settings, you can use plants to soften the paving edge or use broken or small-unit paving, which can be laid to follow gentle curves. In a wildlife garden, you could lay the turf right up to the water's edge or create a beach effect with large pebbles so that birds and other wild creatures can bathe and drink with ease. Turfing to the edge of ordinary ponds is not recommended because soil and clippings will inevitably fall in and foul the water.

Creating a bog garden

A bog garden contains permanently moist soil and enables you to grow plants that are well-adapted to such conditions. Bog gardens associate well with water features such as ponds and streams, helping to integrate them into the wider garden. They can also make an attractively lush feature in their own right. Mid-spring is an ideal time to make a new bog garden.

Making a bog garden

If you are making a garden pond using a flexible liner it is easy to extend the excavation to create a depression 45cm (18in) deep for the bog garden. All you need to do is buy a liner that is large enough to cover both areas and lay it on a bed of sand. The liner covering the bottom of the bog garden needs to be perforated with a few holes and lined with a layer of gravel 5cm (2in) deep for drainage. Build a low wall of stones to separate the pond from the bog area, and lay some fine-mesh netting along the bog garden side of the stones to prevent the soil washing into the pond. Half-fill the bog garden with soil mixture made from 75 per cent

Bog gardens work particularly well alongside water features such as this gurgle pond, but can make attractive features in their own right too.

loam and 25 per cent well-rotted organic matter. Lay some decorative pebbles to conceal the netting, then top up the bog garden with soil mix that's had a little balanced slow-release fertilizer mixed in. Trim the edge of the liner to leave a 15cm (6in) overlap all the way around, and

cover this with pebbles or with a layer of soil or turf. If you don't have a pond, you can create a bog garden in the same way using perforated pond liner. You can also create a bog garden adjacent to an existing water feature, but take care not to undermine the feature.

PLANTING A BOG GARDEN

1 Adjust the position of the bog plants while they are still in their pots until you are satisfied with the arrangement. Cultivate the soil carefully, avoiding any subterranean liner, and remove any perennial weeds complete with roots.

2 Water each container well and allow to drain before planting the centre of the bog garden first. Make a planting hole and set the plant as it was in the container.

3 Firm the soil carefully around each plant. Level the soil over the bog garden after planting is complete and cover the surface with a layer of loose organic mulch to help prevent moisture loss and keep down weeds.

Good bog garden plants

Aruncus	Ligularia
Astilbe	Lobelia
Caltha	cardinalis
Cardamine	Lysichiton
Filipendula	Lythrum
Hemerocallis	Matteuccia
Hosta	Primula
Houttuynia	Rodgersia
Iris ensata	Schizostylis
Iris sibirica	Trollius
Juncus effusus	Zantedeschia

Planting boggy ground

If you have a naturally boggy garden, you can grow bog garden plants throughout. Because bog gardens over 1.8m (6ft) wide are difficult to maintain, consider running a pathway through the area. On a small scale, stepping-stone logs would be adequate, but over larger areas consider installing a raised walkway made from timber decking materials. If pressure-treated with preservative to prevent rotting, they'll last many years even with their supports in soggy soil. Along the edges of your bog garden, grow moisture-loving shrubs or make a backdrop from willow canes, which will root to form a living screen.

All bog gardens need regular watering in dry spells, so it is always worth laying a seep hose on the soil surface before you plant. Once planting has been completed, cover the seep hose with a layer of mulch so that it is out of sight.

MAKING A PEBBLE FOUNTAIN

1 Mark out the diameter of the reservoir and dig a hole slightly wider and deeper than its dimensions. Place a shallow layer of sand at the bottom. Make sure that the reservoir rim is slightly below the level of the surrounding soil so that water will drain naturally into it.

2 Backfill the gap between the reservoir and the sides of the hole with soil. Firm in. Create a catchment area by sloping the surrounding soil slightly towards the rim of the reservoir. Place two bricks at the bottom to act as a plinth for the pump. Then position the pump.

3 Ensure the pipe used for the fountain spout will be 5–8cm (2–3in) higher than the sides of the reservoir. Line the catchment area with a plastic sheet and either cut it so the plastic drapes into the reservoir or cut a hole in the centre for the fountain pipe. Fill with water.

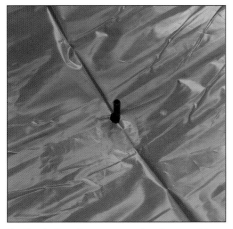

4 Check that the pump works, then position the plastic sheet over the reservoir, with the fountain pipe protruding through the hole. Fit the fountain spout. Weigh down the edges of the sheet to keep it in place as you work.

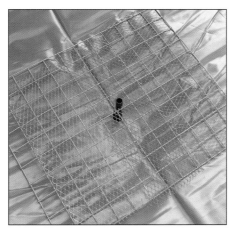

5 Place a piece of heavy-duty galvanized mesh (large enough to rest on the rim of the reservoir) on top to support the weight of large cobbles. Place a finer mesh on top of the larger one to prevent smaller stones falling through.

6 Cover the area around the pump with a layer of cobbles. Check the height of the spout is satisfactory. When you are happy with the fountain, finish arranging the cobbles so that the spout is hidden.

Creating a rock garden

A rock garden will allow you to enjoy a greater range of plants than you might otherwise be able to grow in your garden. It is best sited in a sunny, open location away from overhanging trees, and can look especially good alongside a water feature. Rock gardens are often a convenient way of turning an awkward slope into an attractive focal point but work equally well on the flat if the rocks are carefully positioned so that they look like a natural rocky outcrop.

Choosing materials

The rocks you choose will, to a large extent, be dictated by what's available in your area. Check your *Yellow Pages* for local quarries and specialist suppliers. Stick to only one type of rock that has clearly defined strata running through it and a texture and colour that will suit its surroundings. Most rock gardens are constructed from limestone or sandstone, but slate and other types of rock can also be used to good effect. As a rule of thumb,

you'll need about 1 tonne (1 ton) of rock per square metre (yard) of rock garden. Don't be tempted to buy large rocks unless you have means of moving them into position.

Building the rock garden

Plan your rock garden carefully. Once the rock has been delivered, inspect each piece to find the best 'face' and then work out how you are going to position them. The crucial point when building a rockery is to make it look as natural as possible

MAKING A ROCK GARDEN

1 Dig out the base of the rockery and fill it with a free-draining hardcore. The base of the rock garden is a good place to dispose of all the rubble and subsoil that will have been excavated if you have dug out a pond.

2 Use a special soil mixture for the top 15–23cm (6–9in), especially if soil excavated from the pond is used. Mix equal parts of soil, sharp sand or grit and peat substitute and spread it evenly over the mound.

3 Lay the first rocks at the base of the site, making sure that the strata run in the same direction, and add more soil mixture around them. Repeat the process until the first layer of rocks has been completed.

4 Lever the next row of rocks into position. If you are working alone, rollers and levers are the best way to move heavy rocks around. Again, align the strata lines with those of the first layer of stones.

5 As each layer is built up, add more of the soil mixture and consolidate it around each of the rocks in turn so that they cannot move. Leave for two weeks to allow the soil to settle and top up if necessary.

6 Make sure that the sides slope inwards and make the top reasonably flat rather than building it into a pinnacle. Position the plants, then cover the exposed soil with a layer of fine stone chippings or gravel.

PLANTING A ROCK GARDEN

1 Position the plants while they are still in their pots so that you can see how they look and adjust if necessary. Alpine species are a good choice of plant for a rock garden.

2 Use a trowel to take out a hole a little larger than the rootball. You can buy narrow trowels that are particularly useful for planting in the crevices between rocks.

3 Finish off by covering the exposed surface with more grit to improve drainage and to protect leaves from splashing mud.

and not appear like a spoil heap, studded with rocks. To achieve a natural effect, you will need to angle each rock so that the strata lines all run in the same direction. On a flat site, try positioning the rocks like a natural outcrop with the lines of strata at a 45-degree angle. Or lay flattish stones on the surface to create a craggy pavement effect. Most alpines and rock garden plants prefer a well-drained soil, so you will have to prepare the site thoroughly. First dig out the topsoil and replace it with a 15cm (6in) layer of hardcore for drainage. Mix the topsoil with equal parts of sharp sand or grit and well-rotted leafmould or peat substitute. Place the soil mix on top of the drainage material and then position the rocks (see left). Leave plenty of soil mix to one side for filling in between and behind the rocks once they are positioned. Once construction is complete, leave for two weeks to allow the soil to settle and then make any adjustments needed and top up gaps with soil mix. Plant up the rockery and then cover the surface between the plants with a 1cm (½in) layer of stone chippings that should blend in with the rocks.

Rock gardens associate particularly well with ponds and other water features. Here, the rocky outcrops provide a natural setting for a simple water cascade and pool.

Planting a hanging basket

The best hanging baskets are those planted with fairly small plants that are then grown on in a light, frost-free place until it is safe to put them outdoors – perhaps in late spring or early summer. A greenhouse is ideal, but you might also be able to use an enclosed or protected porch. Giving the baskets protection for a few weeks enables the plants to recover from being transplanted before they have to contend with the more exposed conditions outdoors.

Practical matters

Larger hanging baskets are easier to look after and produce far better displays, so choose the largest your hanging basket bracket can hold – ideally 45cm (18in) in diameter. There are basically two types of basket: those made from open wire mesh and those with solid plastic sides. Traditionally, baskets were made from plastic-coated wire mesh that was lined with sphagnum moss with plants poking through holes in the mesh and cascading over the rim.

Reliable basket plants

Foliage	Petunia
Cineraria	Portulaca
Glechoma	Scaevola
Hedera	Tagetes
Helichrysum	Verbena
petiolare	Viola
Lysimachia	
Plectranthus	Trailers
	Anagallis
Flowers	Convolvulus
Begonia	sabatius
Bidens	Diascia
Brachyscome	Fuchsia
Felicia	Lotus
Gazania	Pelargonium
Heliotrope	(ivy-leaved)
Impatiens	Sanvitalia
Osteospermum	Sutera
Pelargonium	Tropaeolum

Solid-sided baskets are planted only in the top so that the container is never completely hidden from view.

Watering hanging baskets is the critical maintenance task through the summer months. Wire-mesh baskets are more difficult to keep moist because water is lost through the sides, although this can be partially overcome by lining the bottom of the basket with plastic or placing a saucer in the basket (to act as a water reservoir) before adding the compost (soil mix). Some solid-sided plastic baskets also have a special reservoir built into the base, making them even easier to keep moist. Another option is to add water-retaining granules to the compost before you plant or to use a special hanging basket formula that has enhanced water-holding capacity. Either will mean you can leave more time between waterings. Don't be tempted to use more than the recommended amount, and check first that the compost does not already contain a water-retaining

PLANTING A HANGING BASKET

1 Stand the basket on a large pot or a bucket to keep it stable while you are filling the basket. Carefully place the liner in position so that it fills the basket. Pierce a few holes in the bottom.

2 Half-fill the liner with compost (soil mix), then mix in some hydrated water-retaining granules to help prevent the basket from drying out. Add some slow-release fertilizer to feed plants throughout the summer.

3 Cut holes 4cm (1½in) across in the sides of the liner. Wrap the plant in a small piece of plastic and carefully poke it through the hole. Remove the plastic, loosen the rootball and add more compost mixture.

4 Plant up the rest of the basket, packing the plants much more tightly together than you would in the open ground. Top up with compost and water well. Keep the basket under cover until all risk of frost has passed.

substance, since excessive amounts can cause the compost to froth up.

Wire-mesh hanging baskets need to be lined before the compost is added. Traditionally, a 5cm (2in) layer of sphagnum moss was used, but today this is rejected by many gardeners on environmental grounds. Consequently, recycled materials, such as wool, cotton and coconut fibre, have become popular, or you could opt for pre-formed liners made from other materials, including compressed paper and polystyrene foam. Make sure you choose one that looks attractive so that it doesn't detract from your basket displays early in the season. Most man-made liners can be reused for more than one season if you do not damage them when you empty the basket in the autumn. Another option is to use materials from your garden. For example, moss raked from the lawn can be used as long as you haven't treated the grass with chemicals recently, and trimmings from conifer hedges make attractive, long-lasting evergreen liners for winter baskets.

Planting a wire basket takes more time and skill than a solid plastic

Orange pansies planted with daisy-like *Brachyscome* and trailing convolvulus make a delightful combination, and if watered and fed regularly should provide a display that lasts all summer.

USING WATER-RETAINING GRANULES

1 For those that need pre-hydrating, pour the recommended amount of water into a bowl. Add the granules, stirring occasionally until they have absorbed the water.

2 Add the hydrated granules to compost (soil mix) at the recommended rate. Mix the hydrated granules thoroughly with the compost before using the mixture for planting.

one to get right. Use trailing plants in the sides and around the rim, with more upright plants in the top. When planting the sides, you may find it best to push the plants out from the inside so that the rootball is not damaged. Alternatively, roll up the rootball in a small piece of plastic before sliding it carefully through the hole. Once the plant is in the right position, simply pull off the plastic. To make watering easier, push a small, empty pot into the top of the basket after planting and fill it with stones. Then, apply water into the pot so that the water can gradually soak into the compost.

Sowing flowers

Biennials, such as wallflowers and forget-me-nots, are easy to raise from seed, and because they can be sown direct outdoors they need very little attention. Border perennials, such as lupins and aquilegias, are also easily raised from seed sown now, and many of them will flower next summer. Others may take another year or so to become established before flowering.

What is a biennial?

Biennials are plants that grow and establish in the first year, then flower, set seed and die in the second year. There are many good and popular flowering biennials that can be sown in late spring or early summer. Now is the time to sow double daisies, forget-me-nots, wallflowers, polyanthus, sweet Williams, Iceland poppies and sweet rocket (see right). One of the main advantages of growing hardy biennials is that they are sown after the spring rush is over and you don't need to provide any expensive equipment. Biennials also flower at useful times. Early types, such as polyanthus and winter pansies, can be in bloom during late winter if weather conditions are kind, while the double daisies and forget-me-nots add much to the spring displays. But plants such as

Biennial selector

Name	sowing time	flowering period
Anchusa	early summer	late winter – late summer
Brompton stock	early summer	late spring – midsummer
Canterbury bell	mid-spring	late spring – midsummer
Double daisy	late spring	early spring – midsummer
Evening primrose	early summer	early summer – mid-autumn
Forget-me-not	late spring	early spring – early summer
Foxglove	early summer	early summer – midsummer
Honesty	early summer	mid-spring – early summer
Iceland poppy	late spring	early summer – late summer
Pansies, winter	early summer	late winter – midsummer
Polyanthus	late spring	late winter – early summer
Sweet rocket	mid-spring	early summer
Sweet William	late spring	early summer – midsummer
Verbascum	mid-spring	early summer – late summer
Wallflower	late spring	mid-spring – early summer

SOWING BIENNIALS AND HARDY PERENNIALS

1 Prepare the ground thoroughly, and make sure that you remove all traces of perennial weeds and their roots. Break the soil down into a fine, crumbly structure once it has been cleared of weeds.

2 Take out drills with the corner of a hoe or rake to the recommended depth (this varies with the seed, so check the packet). The drills can be quite close together, because the seedlings will be transplanted later.

3 Run water into the drill before sowing if the soil is dry. Space the seeds thinly, and as evenly as you can. This makes thinning and later transplanting much easier.

4 Cover the seeds carefully by easing the soil back with the back of a rake, taking care that you do not disturb the seeds. Remember to add a label.

5 Thin the seedlings as soon as they are large enough to handle easily so that they do not become overcrowded. Remove the weakest seedlings without uprooting those left behind.

the late-spring-flowering Brompton stocks and sweet Williams are the most useful, because they can be used as gap fillers – they can cover any spaces that are left behind by spring-flowering bulbs as well as provide temporary cover between new shrubs and perennials in a recently planted bed.

Raising from seedlings

If you need to raise a lot of plants, sow directly into a prepared seedbed (see opposite). Thin out the seedlings as soon as they are large enough to separate, and plant out into their final positions during mid-autumn. For just a few plants, or if your soil is very heavy, you can also raise biennials in seed trays and pots – just like bedding plants. This method is particularly worthwhile for late-winter-flowering biennials, such as winter pansies and polyanthus, which need optimum growing conditions to develop into sturdy plants. Prick out and pot up the seedlings into individual containers and stand them outside, making sure they get plenty of water during the summer. Feed every couple of weeks with a dilute liquid fertilizer. Plant out in mid-autumn, spacing plants about 15–45cm (6–18in) apart, depending on how big the plants grow.

Make sure the beds are weed-free before planting out – if any perennial weed roots remain, it will be difficult to dig them out without disturbing the plants. It is best to remove new weeds by hand as they appear – avoid using a hoe as it is likely to damage the plants. Covering the soil with a mulch of organic material will help prevent weeds germinating, and will also improve soil structure and fertility as it is incorporated.

Sweet Williams (*Dianthus barbatus*) are a short-lived perennial, grown as a biennial. They come in a range of pinks, white and bicoloured, and as the name suggests, they are sweetly scented.

BETTER FLOWERING DISPLAYS

1 Deadheading Regularly remove fading flowerheads to encourage repeat-flowering plants to produce a succession of new blooms over a longer period.

2 Feeding An application of high-potash fertilizer during the growing season will help promote better flowering. If using a granular feed, take care not to get any on the leaves.

3 Mulching A layer of composted bark or garden compost will help suppress weeds and conserve moisture. As the worms take it down, it will also improve the soil.

4 Pinching out Keep plants compact by pinching or cutting out the central growing tip to encourage sideshoots to develop, making for more bushy growth.

Caring for trees and shrubs

Late spring is a good time to take stock of your shrubs and trees and check that they are providing good value for money when you consider the space they occupy. Those that have outgrown their allotted space can be earmarked for pruning back in autumn, although a few can be tackled now using the one-in-three pruning method. Once flowering is over, shrubs such as ceanothus, olearia and philadelphus that may have become overgrown can be cut back by removing the oldest and thickest stems. By repeating the process after flowering each year for three years, you will have completely rejuvenated the shrub without losing the entire flowering display.

A large rhododendron like this can have its season of interest extended by growing a climber through it. A good choice might be an early-flowering clematis, such as *Clematis alpina,* which will flower before the (deciduous) rhododendron is in full leaf, and is not so vigorous as to overwhelm its host.

Improving trees and shrubs

You can also improve the display of an established tree or shrub by planting a suitable climber next to it and training the climber to scramble through the canopy of foliage. For best results, choose a complementary climber that matches the vigour of its host and produces its flowers at a time when the host does not, in order to extend the overall display. The host should have a framework that is strong enough to bear the weight of the climber and should not be too young or too old. Do not try to brighten the display of an old and exhausted host because you will simply hasten its demise.

Position the climber on the side of the prevailing wind, so that its stems will be blown against the supporting host and not away from it. Plant the climber in the 'drip zone' just under the edge of the canopy of the host so that any water that runs off the foliage during downpours falls where the climber can make use of it. If the host is very large and well established with lots of roots near the surface, you will need to protect the climber from competition with its host. Dig a large hole, removing any perennial weeds and tree or shrub roots as you go, add plenty of well-rotted organic matter, and plant the climber. You can line the sides of the planting hole with sheets of strong plastic to allow the climber a free root-run. With a shrub host, drive in a cane next to the climber, angled towards the shrub, tie the top to the shrub and train the climber along it. With

'Zéphirine Drouhin' is a beautiful, repeat-flowering climbing Bourbon rose that's excellent for covering a wall (whether sunny or not) or growing through an established large shrub or tree.

Groundcover selector

Ajuga reptans	*procumbens*
Alchemilla mollis	*Geranium*
Berberis	*Hebe pinguifolia*
thunbergii	'Pagei'
Bergenia	*Hedera helix*
Brunnera	*Hosta*
macrophylla	*Juniperus* ×
Calluna vulgaris	*media*
Clematis cirrhosa	*Lamium*
'Balearica'	*maculatum*
Clematis	*Nepeta* ×
flammula	*fassenii*
Cotoneaster	*Pachysandra*
'Coral Beauty'	*terminalis*
Epimedium	*Persicaria affinis*
perralderianum	*Pulmonaria*
Euonymus	*saccharata*
fortunei	Roses,
Gaultheria	groundcover

a tree, it is best to tie the climber to a secure stake, and tie a rope from the stake to the canopy of the tree. This will greatly reduce the danger of the climber being pulled out of the ground whenever the tree sways in a strong gust of wind.

Adding groundcover

The space underneath established trees and shrubs can also be improved using climbers as groundcover. Again choose a complementary partner that will enhance the existing display. Between trees you can use fast-growing climbers such as some types of clematis and honeysuckle or large-leaved, variegated ivies, such as *Hedera colchica* 'Dentata Variegata'. The area between shrubs could be improved with less vigorous clematis or with small-leaved decorative ivies. Ivies are particularly useful because they are evergreen and because it is easy to remove unwanted stems. Add spring-flowering bulbs to come up through the ground-covering climbers to extend the flowering interest into another season.

PLANTING A CLIMBER NEXT TO AN ESTABLISHED SHRUB

1 Improve the appearance of a dull shrub by adding a climbing companion. Choose one that does not flower at the same time as the shrub.

2 Dig a hole at the edge of the supporting shrub so that the climber will receive rain. Improve the soil if necessary, and plant the climber, angled towards the shrub.

3 Using a cane, train the climber, such as this clematis, into the shrub. Spread out the shoots so that it grows evenly throughout the shrub.

4 Water the new plant thoroughly and mulch around the plant to conserve moisture in the soil. Continue to water, especially in dry weather, until the climber is established.

Stocking your pond

This is a good time to plant up your pond, whether you are establishing a new one or just adding some new plants to an existing one. For a pond to look good for much of the year and to remain largely self-reliant you need to choose the plants carefully, selecting the right combination of well-behaved species that will suit your size of pond.

Planting a pool

Pond plants are categorized according to the position they occupy in the pond.

• Deep-water plants, such as waterlilies, help to cover the surface with foliage, providing much-needed shade for fish and discouraging the growth of algae.

• Decorative marginal plants are positioned in the shallows, at the edge of a pond, with their roots in water and their topgrowth above it.

• Submerged aquatics, such as elodea, are efficient at releasing oxygen into the water, which helps to keep it healthy for fish and other wildlife.

PLANTING MARGINAL AQUATICS

1 If you are using a planting basket that does not have micro-mesh lining, line it with hessian sacking before filling it with aquatic compost (soil mix).

2 Remove the plant from its container and plant it in the basket at its original depth, using a trowel to add or remove compost as necessary. Firm it in well.

3 Cover with gravel to help keep the soil in place when you position the container in the pond, and to reduce the risk of it being disturbed by fish.

4 Soak the planted basket before placing it on the shelf at the edge of the pool. The top of the basket should be 2.5–5cm (1–2in) below the water surface.

One of the best-loved pond plants, waterlilies not only produce a succession of beautiful flowers, but their leaves provide shade that discourages the formation of algae.

Some oxygenating or submerged plants are sold as cuttings bundled together, perhaps weighted so that they sink. Some are very decorative, such as water crowfoot, which produces feathery submerged growth and occasional cup-shaped, golden-centred, white flowers on the surface, or water violet, which bears upright spikes of lilac flowers in summer. Simply throw them into the pond.

Deep-water plants are easiest to grow in specially designed planting baskets. The baskets are often square, so that they fit neatly together, and are flat-bottomed to make them stable. Traditional lattice-sided baskets must be lined with hessian sacking before planting to

PLANTING A WATERLILY

1 Planting baskets are the best option, but for deep-water plants such as waterlilies you can use a washing-up bowl. Make holes in the bottom and line it with sacking before adding aquatic compost (soil mix).

2 Never add ordinary fertilizers as these are likely to encourage a proliferation of algae that will turn the water green. Instead, use a special fertilizer, sold specifically for aquatic plants.

3 Remove the waterlily from its container, and plant in the bowl at its original depth. Top up with aquatic compost as necessary, gently firming the compost as you do so.

4 Add a layer of gravel to prevent the compost washing out or being disturbed by fish as they search for food. The gravel also weighs down the container.

5 Soak the container by standing it in a bucket or bowl and flooding it from the top. This will help to prevent compost from washing out later.

6 Place the bowl in a shallow part of the pond initially, especially if new leaves are just developing. Alternatively, raise it up on bricks in deeper water.

prevent the compost (soil mix) from washing out, but modern aquatic containers have micro-mesh sides. Growing your pond plants in aquatic baskets allows you to move the plants around and take them out easily when necessary.

It is important to use aquatic compost that has been specially formulated for pond plants. The plant nutrients in ordinary compost are too easily leached out into the surrounding water, which encourages algal growth. After planting, top up the basket with a 2cm (¾in) layer of pea gravel to prevent the compost from washing out of the basket and making the water muddy. Soak each planted basket thoroughly in a

bucket of water to remove any air bubbles before carefully lowering it into the pond.

If your pond has very narrow marginal shelves that cannot accommodate standard containers, try making a planting container from an old pair of tights (pantyhose). Insert one leg inside the other to form a tube that has double sides. Fill this with aquatic compost and tie at the end. Make small holes in the top to plant through and tie up the holes afterwards so that the compost cannot escape. Then mould the planting sausage to the shape of your pond.

When you buy waterlilies, they will have been raised in shallow water

so the leaves (or lily pads) will have short stems. This means that the plant will need to be raised up on an up-turned pot or, depending on the depth of your pond, bricks for a couple of weeks so that the leaves float on the surface. Lower the container in the pond week by week until it is resting on the bottom.

Introducing fish

First, acclimatize the fish to their new environment by floating the plastic bag that you transported them in on the surface of the water for an hour. This will allow the water temperatures to equalize gradually, then the fish can swim out of the bag. Never put fish directly into the pond.

Planting permanent containers

You don't have to spend a lot of money each year filling containers with bedding plants and tender perennials to get a colourful display. There are many hardy plants that will do the job for you year after year with the minimum of maintenance. Containers also give you the opportunity to try out plant combinations on a small scale before using them in the open garden.

Practical matters

Although many perennials are not well suited to growing in containers, there is a good selection that will thrive and make attractive easy-care patio plants. Because perennials are generally deeper rooted and more vigorous than bedding plants, they will need larger containers if you want a long-term, trouble-free display. To prevent the most vigorous plants overwhelming the others, grow the plants in individual pots that can be grouped together to form an attractive display on the patio. This is a good way of growing invasive perennials, such as variegated ground elder, which would otherwise run riot in beds and borders. Include plants with attractive foliage in your collection to extend the period of interest, and

Perennials for containers

Small containers	Pulmonaria
Ajuga	Sempervivum
Alchemilla	**Large containers**
Aquilegia	Acanthus
Bellis	Agapanthus
Bergenia	Astilbe
Diascia	Dicentra
Erigeron	Euphorbia
Ferns (hardy)	Geranium
Festuca	Hemerocallis
Hakonechloa	Hosta
Lamium	Leucanthemum
Ophiopogon	Sedum

combine plants that flower at different times, because hardy perennials do not flower for as long as traditional bedding plants.

Any type of container will do provided it is at least 30cm (12in) across, ideally 45cm (18in), with several drainage holes. To reduce watering, use plastic pots that do not lose moisture through their sides, or line porous containers, such as terracotta pots, with plastic sheeting before you plant (taking care not to cover the drainage holes). Cover the drainage holes with crocks or stones to prevent the compost (soil mix) washing out and fill the container with a loam-based formula, such as John Innes No. 2. Unlike peat-based composts, loam-based types maintain their structure over many years, and being heavier, they also make the container more stable.

Shrubs in tubs

Many shrubs can be grown more or less permanently in large containers. Choose types that can tolerate a restricted root-run and that grow relatively slowly. Many conifers are ideal because they provide year-round appeal, but you can also grow other evergreens, such as bay, box, lavender,

PLANTING A SHRUB IN A TUB

1 Choose a large tub or pot with an inside diameter of at least 45cm (18in), unless you are planting a very small shrub. A heavy clay or stone container will be more stable than plastic for top-heavy plants. Cover the drainage holes with pieces of broken pots.

2 Part-fill the tub or pot with a loam-based compost (soil mix). Knock the plant from its pot, and if the roots are tightly wound around the rootball tease some of them out so they will grow into the surrounding compost more readily.

3 Add or remove compost as necessary, so that the top of the rootball and soil level will be 2.5–5cm (1–2in) below the rim of the pot to allow for watering. Make sure the shrub is upright before adding compost around the sides.

4 Backfill the compost around the roots firmly, because trees and shrubs offer a great deal of wind resistance. Water thoroughly after planting. Thereafter, water as necessary, including during the winter months.

rosemary and spotted laurel. Flowering shrubs are a better choice if you want to make a splash at a particular time of year. Dwarf rhododendrons and deciduous azaleas light up the spring patio, as do colourful camellias. These plants must be grown in acid conditions, so choose an ericaceous formula and water with saved rainwater. Growing these shrubs in tubs means that you can even grow them successfully in a garden with chalky (alkaline) soil. However, for an ever-changing, attractive display you need look no further than the coral bark maple (*Acer palmatum* 'Sango-kaku'), which has attractive foliage all summer, fiery autumn colour and stunning winter bark.

If you have somewhere you can keep your container plants protected in winter, you can extend the range of shrubs you grow in your garden by choosing tender exotics for your containers. Try the ferny-leaved mimosa (*Acacia dealbata*), which bears clouds of yellow flowers, or a member of the citrus family for a crop of oranges, lemons or limes.

Fuchsias will grow very successfully in containers, producing their beautiful flowers over a long period. Hardy varieties can stay outside all year in most gardens.

PLANTING A CLIMBER IN A HALF-BARREL

1 Fill a half-barrel with a loam-based compost (soil mix). You need a large, deep container and heavy compost, which will hold the canes securely as well as the plants.

2 Choose a climber to suit the size of the container. For instance, in a barrel of this size, you could grow three or four non-vigorous clematis. Angle the plants together.

3 Tie the canes together with string or use a proprietary plastic cane holder. When the growth reaches the top, it will tumble down again and make the planting look even denser.

Planting your patio

Pots and tubs can make superb displays on the patio, but there are other opportunities in and around the patio you can take advantage of. If your paving looks a bit stark there are a number of ways you can soften the edges and break up the harsh-looking appearance. This is especially desirable if you want to create an informal, cottage garden feel in the patio.

Introducing plant material

Around the edges you could create planting pockets by removing one or two paving stones and replacing the hardcore with soil before planting (see below). Choose an area that is not much used and that is well away from the points of access. Some species are so well adapted to growing in the harsh conditions found on a sun-drenched patio that even quite small cracks and crevices can be planted successfully.

Planting cracks

Look out for cracks between paving that are colonized by weeds, because these will provide ideal conditions for growing drought-tolerant, low-growing plants that are tough enough to be walked on occasionally. Filling cracks with plants prevents them being recolonized by weeds and eliminates the need to spend time on weeding. Choose plants that produce ground-hugging, dense growth that doesn't get too woody, so that they do not become a safety hazard for anyone using the patio. Most thymes are ideal because they also fill the air with a pleasing aroma when they are gently crushed underfoot.

Prepare the cracks by removing or killing the existing crop of weeds. The easiest way with firmly-lodged perennial weeds is to use a spot weedkiller that will kill the roots. Clear out as much debris as you can from the crack using a patio weed hook or an old screwdriver. The deeper you can go the better so that any new plant will have more rooting space to become established. Trickle a loam-based compost (soil mix) into the crack, poking it in to remove any air pockets.

The easiest way to plant a crack is to sow seeds thinly, then dust with sieved compost before watering with a fine spray that doesn't wash away the seed. When the seedlings are large enough to handle, they need to be thinned, leaving the strongest seedlings at their final spacing. In wider cracks you can plant with small plug plants that have a wedge-shaped rootball that will slot easily into the crack. If the rootball is too wide, gently compress it between the

Plants for paving

Cracks
Aubrieta deltoidea
Dianthus deltoides
Erinus alpinus
Mentha requienii
Scabiosa graminifolia
Thymus serpyllum
Crevices
Globularia cordifolia
Lewisia tweedyi
Saxifraga callosa
Sedum spathulifolium
Sempervivum
Thymus
Planting pockets
Armeria juniperifolia
Campanula carpatica
Cerastium tomentosum
Chamaemelum nobile
Erica carnea
Iberis sempervirens
Origanum dictamnus
Sedum telephium
Veronica prostrata

PLANTING THE PATIO

1 Lift one or two paving slabs, depending on their size. If they have been mortared into position, loosen the slabs with a cold chisel and club hammer, then lever them up with a chisel or crowbar.

2 If the paving slab has been bedded on concrete, break this up with a cold chisel and club hammer. Remove the rubble and fork over the soil, adding well-rotted garden compost or manure and a slow-release fertilizer.

3 Plant the shrub or climber, firming it in well and watering thoroughly. Arrange decorative pebbles or gravel over the soil to make the feature more attractive and reduce the chance of the soil splashing on to the paving.

palms of your hands until it is narrow enough to slot in.

Planting crevices

Crevices in walls can be tackled in a similar way. You may have to enlarge the hole to take the rootball and compost by drilling or chipping at the edges with a club hammer and cold chisel. Fill the prepared hole with loam-based compost. Ideally, the crevice should be angled downwards so that the compost is not washed out by rain. If necessary, lodge a stone at the entrance to prevent the compost falling out. Sow or plant the crevice in the same way as cracks in paving (see above).

Once the cracks and crevices have been planted (or seedlings thinned), cover the surface of the compost with a layer of stone chippings or

PLANTING CRACKS AND CREVICES

1 Chisel out spaces in your paving at least 5cm (2in) deep and remove as much of the rubble as possible. Add loam-based compost (soil mix) and sow or plant as appropriate. Water regularly, using a fine mist sprayer to avoid washing the compost away.

2 Press moist loam-based compost into a crevice using a small dibber or your fingers. Firm in to avoid air pockets. Insert the plant and add more compost. Keep the compost moist by spraying with a fine mist until the plants become established.

grit to prevent the compost being colonized by weeds before the plants become established. The grit mulch will also help maintain soil moisture

around the roots of the plants. Water well after planting and keep watering until the plants are well established.

Soften the harsh outline of your patio by planting up pockets, cracks and crevices with suitable plants. Here, herbs such as thyme are used to good effect, as they are allowed to form neat mats of fragrant foliage and flowers.

Topiary and alpine troughs

There is a growing fashion for topiary these days, and ready-clipped shrubs are sold in every conceivable shape, from simple spheres and cones to sculptured racing cars and patio sets. Because topiary is usually created using very slow-growing plants, such as box (*Buxus*), the finished article is not cheap, especially if you choose one of the larger, more complex shapes.

Going it alone

Topiary needn't cost the earth if you are prepared to do it yourself – and it can be highly rewarding. It needn't take forever, either, since you can use faster-growing plants, such as some species of conifers, if you don't mind clipping them frequently, or make a mock-topiary using a quick-growing evergreen climber, such as small-leaved ivy, trained over a wire frame (see below).

Traditional topiary is easy to create if you have the patience. A young box plant can be clipped into shape over a number of years to create almost any form you like. Formal shapes such as spheres and cones are the easiest because you can use canes and wires to provide accurate guides when you trim. More elaborate designs will require an artistic eye and a good deal of creative skill if they are to look

Topiary has a long tradition in Japan, with highly stylized shapes that can take many years to perfect.

MAKING AN IVY STANDARD

1 Choose an ivy that has pliable stems, such as *Hedera maroccana* 'Spanish Canary'. Insert a broom handle or cane into a pot filled with loam-based compost (soil mix) and place the plants at even intervals around its base.

2 Working from bottom to top, carefully wrap the stems around the broom handle or cane, tying the stems together with twists or split rings at regular intervals, to create a braided effect around the cane.

3 As you get higher up the broom handle or cane, take care to check that the stems cross each time in a straight line above the previous crossed stems, and that the regular spacing is maintained throughout.

4 Take a 25cm (10in) wire hanging basket and place it upside down on top of the broom handle or cane. Fix it securely in place with staples, wire or nails so that the weight of the plant won't dislodge it.

5 Wind the tops of the shoots through the wire basket and snip off all the lower leaves using scissors. As the ivy continues to grow, train the shoots through the basket, covering the frame completely.

Plants for traditional topiary

Berberis	*Ligustrum*
Buxus	*ovalifolium*
Crataegus	*Lonicera nitida*
Cupressus	*Myrtus*
sempervirens	*communis*
Hedera	*Osmanthus*
Ilex	*Prunus lusitanica*
Juniperus	*Santolina*
communis	*chamae-*
Laurus	*cyparissus*
nobilis	*Taxus*

PLANTING A TROUGH

1 Place the trough in its final position before it is filled; otherwise, it will be too heavy to move. It must be in a warm, sunny spot. Troughs look best when they are raised on bricks or concrete blocks. Make sure it is stable and will not tip over.

2 Make sure that the trough is level and has adequate drainage holes. Place coarse drainage material over the drainage holes and over the base of the trough to a depth of about 5cm (2in). Pieces of broken pot, brick or other rubble are all suitable.

3 Top the drainage material with a suitable free-draining alpine compost (soil mix), adding it in layers and making sure that it is firmed in thoroughly, especially in the corners and around the edge. Fill to within 2.5cm (1in) of the top.

4 Decorate the surface with attractive pieces of rock. Angle the pieces into the compost, making sure that about one-third of each piece is buried to create mini-outcrops that will provide various pockets for planting a selection of alpines.

5 Plant the selected alpines in the trough, scooping out holes to take the rootball of each in turn. Firm the plants in but avoid the temptation to over-firm. Place the larger and central plants first, finishing with smaller ones around the edges.

6 Finish off with a top-dressing of coarse grit or rock chippings, pushed well under the topgrowth of each alpine. Keep well watered at first, but avoid wetting the leaves unnecessarily. Once established, the trough should need only occasional watering.

convincing. However, you can make the job easier by growing the plant up through a pre-formed shape made out of chicken wire. It will not be pleasing on the eye until the plant has grown up through the mesh to hide it from view, but the finished topiary will look all the better for it. As shoots grow through the wire mesh, pinch them out between finger and thumb or periodically trim the shoot tips using a pair of secateurs (pruners). This will encourage more bushy growth that will produce a more solid-looking shape. If the shape you have chosen involves developing growth in particular

directions, select a suitable shoot and tie it in to a wire running in that direction. Again, pinch it out to encourage sideshoots to form and pinch these out in turn to cover the wire guide. Remove the ties after a couple of years when the shoot has turned woody and is fixed in position. Repeat this process until the growth meets at the perimeter of the topiary and the whole mesh frame has been covered.

To keep shapes looking neat they will need clipping several times a year, depending on the vigour of the plant used. In late spring give them their first trim and trim again as

necessary throughout the summer, leaving at least four weeks between cuts, with the last trim in early autumn. If you trim later than this the new growth does not have time to ripen properly before winter and is easily damaged, ruining the overall appearance of the topiary.

Damaged topiary can be repaired, however, by training in a new healthy shoot from lower down and tying it into position. Pinch out as before to encourage bushy growth which will soon fill the gap. You can restore the shape of neglected topiary in spring too. Trim it in stages to restore the overall shape and refine the outline.

Summer

Although most of the hard work has been completed in the spring rush, the garden is still a hive of intense activity during the first few weeks of summer. With the threat of frost passed in all but the coldest regions, it is a time to relax and enjoy your garden. Everything is growing rapidly, in many areas tender plants can be put out, and weeds seem to grow faster than you ever thought possible. The bulk of the sowing and pricking out will have been completed by now, so the challenge is to keep all your new plants growing strongly, making sure they don't go short of water and protecting them from pest and disease attack. Most gardens look their best in early summer when the grass is still looking fresh and flowering is reaching its peak.

There will be something new to delight you nearly every day in the ever-changing displays and your garden enjoyment will be extended into long summer evenings with *al fresco* meals and garden parties.

A well-planted garden will be overflowing with colour by summer. Here *Crocosmia* 'Lucifer' stand out against a backdrop of variegated cannas and golden *Achillea*.

The Summer Garden

Summer is a time when you can relax a little and enjoy the results of all your efforts of the last few months. Bedding plants in borders and containers will be growing rapidly, bringing an abundance of colour to prominent areas of the garden, including patios, window boxes and hanging baskets.

Early Summer

Pests and diseases are as active as ever in early summer. Vigilance and prompt action now will often stop the trouble from spreading, thus avoiding the need for more drastic control measures later. Weeds will also need to be kept under control, and preventing any from flowering and setting seed should be your main priority. Unexpected late frosts can occur and in colder areas they may be almost inevitable, so keep garden fleece to hand to cover up newly planted tender flowers just in case.

Early summer is a good time to top up mulches around the garden. Give the ground a thorough soaking beforehand. It's a good idea to mulch all newly planted specimens, as well as the surface of containers, to help retain soil moisture and prevent competition from weeds. In prominent positions try decorative mulches such as chipped bark or stone chippings and pebbles.

In the greenhouse, watering and feeding are of paramount importance and can take up a lot of time if you have a lot of containers. However, there are steps you

Dahlias, such as this rich orange variety, are an ideal choice for bringing the summer to a colourful end.

can take to reduce the workload such as installing drip or capillary watering aids.

Although there is always plenty of colour at this time of year, you should be prepared for a few weeks when the garden is perhaps not looking its best. Early summer is a transitional period, and there is often an interval between the spring-flowering plants dying back and the peak of colour offered by abundant summer bedding.

Summer bulbs, such as *Lilium martagon*, are an easy way to bring a spectacular display of exotic blooms into your garden.

Herbaceous peonies come in a huge range of colours and forms. Despite flowering relatively briefly, they are well loved for the sheer voluptuousness of their early summer blooms.

Midsummer

This is mainly a time to enjoy your garden, rather than do a lot of physical work in it. Most things are already sown or planted, and the emphasis is on weeding and watering as well as regular deadheading to keep the garden looking tidy and flowering well.

Use a hoe to control annual weeds on bare soil. Choose a warm, dry day so that the weeds wither and die quickly after being hoed off. If perennial weeds are a problem, they should be dug out by hand complete with roots to prevent them resprouting.

Watering is another key job of the season. Concentrate on newly planted specimens and those in containers; established plants can survive long periods without water. When you do water, give a thorough soaking. Watering little and often does more harm than good: more is lost through evaporation and it encourages shallow root growth, making plants less able to tap into deep reserves.

To keep flowering displays looking their best, it is worth deadheading regularly. By removing the fading flowerheads you will not only improve the appearance of the plants, but extend the flowering period of many repeat-flowering favourites, such as roses, and get some perennials to put on a second display later in the summer.

Late Summer

In a good year, late summer can be a time of hot, dry weather, when there is a natural lull in the garden, and the efforts of spring and early summer sowing and planting will be paying dividends so for now you can relax a little. Most of this month's work in the garden involves watering and routine maintenance tasks like mowing, hoeing, and clipping hedges.

Late summer is the traditional time to take a break from work and go away, and you can help your garden survive in your absence by preparing it before you go. If possible, get a neighbour to look in from time to time and carry out essential tasks like watering containers.

It is not too soon to start thinking ahead and making plans for winter. Some popular tender plants, such as pelargoniums and fuchsias, can be propagated from summer cuttings and overwintered as rooted cuttings to use in displays next season. And if you have a greenhouse, you can also sow flowering pot plants, such as cyclamen, cineraria and primulas, to bloom next spring. By the end of summer, you can begin to buy and plant spring-flowering bulbs such as daffodils, hyacinths and crocus, although tulips should be left until late autumn. Specially prepared bulbs are also available that can be forced into bloom early, to provide much-needed colour indoors during the winter months.

Dahlia 'Bishop of Llandaff' and *Crocosmia* 'Lucifer' join forces in this vibrant combination for a fiery border display.

Deadheading and mulching

This is a lovely time in the garden, when every time you step outdoors you are greeted by masses of fresh flowers and foliage, the first results of all the hard work you put in over spring. A little extra attention now will keep that freshness going throughout the season, but don't let the workload spoil your pleasure in this delightful time of year.

Deadheading

Many annuals and perennials will produce better and longer lasting displays if they are regularly deadheaded. Annuals in particular respond to having their faded flowers trimmed off by producing further flushes of bloom. This is because annuals grow, flower, set seed and die in a single growing season. So if you prevent them from setting seed by removing the flowers as they fade, they try again by producing further flushes of flowers. The effect is less marked with perennials but still worthwhile for some species. Many types of bedding plant produce too many flowers to make deadheading worthwhile, but ageratum, dianthus, erigeron, all types of marigolds,

Hardy geraniums can benefit from a heavy trim if they get tatty, because they will produce a neat mound of new growth and may flower again too.

mesembryanthemums, mimulus, osteospermums, pansies, phlox and poppies do perform better. If you do not have time to deadhead all your plants, concentrate on those that will benefit most, and plants in prominent positions, such as in

containers on the patio and beds and borders next to paths or near the house. Deadheading may seem a laborious process, but it allows you to keep a close eye on your plants so that you will spot problems early. There are several methods of deadheading; the one to choose depends on the type of growth the plant makes.

Pinching out Meticulously pinching out individual fading blooms by hand is the best way of deadheading many large-flowered annuals. Pinching off the stem between finger and thumb just behind the flower is the best method for plants that produce branching flowerheads that don't all mature at the same time.

Cutting with scissors Annuals and perennials that produce single flowers on long stems are best deadheaded by cutting at the bottom of the stem with a sharp pair of garden scissors. Scissors are also

DEADHEADING

Where roses bear their flowers in clusters, which is common to the majority of rambling roses, start deadheading by removing any individual faded flowers within the cluster. Single flowers can be removed as they fade.

Once the whole flower cluster has faded, cut back to a strong bud facing the way you wish the stem to grow. Here the leaves nearest the cluster are showing signs of black spot, so cut back to a bud behind the diseased growth.

useful for trimming compact plants that produce huge numbers of very tiny flowers. In this case, simply shear off all the wiry flower stalks once most of them have passed their best.

Using secateurs A few plants produce very thick stems that cannot be cut with a pair of scissors, they are best cut back with secateurs (pruners). Plants that produce flower spikes, such as lupins, should have the flower spike cut back to a sideshoot lower down once the flower is spent. This will encourage the sideshoots to produce a display of their own later in the season.

Using shears With a few perennials, such as hardy geraniums, you can cut the whole plant back after flowering using a pair of shears. These plants tend to look tatty by the middle of the summer, but will put on neat new growth and even a second flush of flowers if they are cut back to ground level after flowering. If you have a lot of soft-stemmed bedding you could even try deadheading with a nylon-line trimmer, but you must take care not to damage the plants too much.

MULCHING WITH CHIPPED BARK

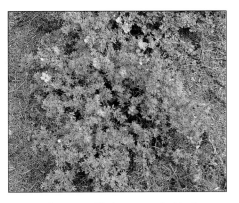

1 Here the potentilla is surrounded by bare earth. Until the bed has been filled with other plants, weeds will be a constant problem, and applying a weed-suppressing mulch will reduce the work needed to keep it clear. The mulch will also make the bed more attractive, as well as conserving moisture in the ground.

After deadheading clear away all of the trimmings and give the plants a thorough watering. If they have been cut back hard, it's also worth giving them a boost by applying a liquid feed. Don't be in a hurry to deadhead all your perennial plants, because some seedheads are worth keeping to provide autumn and winter interest. And if you want to try raising your own plants from seed saved from the garden, you will have to leave some plants to set seed.

2 Chipped or composted bark is a very good mulch. It should be stored for several months to let it release any resin and start to decompose. Some gardeners worry that it introduces fungal diseases, but the spores of these are already in the air and the bark does not appreciably increase the risk.

Mulching

Now is a good time to apply or renew a mulch on the beds to help suppress weeds and conserve moisture. Weed and water the ground first. Composted bark, chipped bark or gravel will set the plants off well. You could also consider using garden compost or leaf mould as a mulch. Other mulches, such as black plastic sheeting, grass clippings and straw, work well but look less attractive.

MULCHING WITH PLASTIC SHEETING

1 Special black plastic, with holes in to allow water to pass through to the soil, is available from garden centres. If you lay the plastic before you plant up the bed, you can cut holes in it and plant through it. Otherwise, you will need to cut it to fit around the existing plants.

2 Plastic would be the perfect mulch were it not so unattractive. However, it can be covered with a layer of gravel or small stones. Make sure the plastic is perfectly flat, with no ridges in it that will poke up through the stones, then pour the gravel on to cover the plastic completely.

3 Gravel makes an ideal background against which to see the plants, and it also looks attractive in its own right. It is easy to maintain and can be simply raked to keep its appearance fresh and level. Make sure that the plastic does not show through, as this can spoil the effect.

Pruning and trimming shrubs

Now that you have more time to stroll around the garden, there is an opportunity to examine and tidy up your permanent plants. Although most shrubs will grow and flower perfectly well without regular pruning, many spring- and early-summer-flowering shrubs benefit from a light trim at this time of the year. It is also not too late to catch up with spring pruning missed through lack of time.

Summer pruning

Without regular attention, some deciduous shrubs will eventually become bare at the base and produce all their flowers out of sight at the top of the plant. Many evergreen shrubs tend to get too big or become lop-sided or mis-shapen. Evergreens grown largely for their ornamental foliage, such as holly and laurel, are usually well-behaved and require little attention. However, low-growing flowering evergreen shrubs, such as lavender, senecio and hebes, can be given a light clipping after flowering to keep them neat and compact. Larger flowering evergreens, such as berberis,

escallonia and viburnum, should not need regular trimming but can be clipped after flowering if required.

Signs of winter damage will be easy to spot at this time of year, and all dead and badly damaged stems should be cut out with secateurs (pruners). Similarly, vigorous all-green shoots produced on variegated plants are easy to identify and must be removed, otherwise they will outgrow and eventually swamp the variegated shoots, spoiling the overall appearance of the shrub.

Light trim

Some shrubs should be trimmed annually during the summer because they do not respond to hard pruning. If you cut them back hard they do not produce new shoots from old wood lower down. By giving them a light trim every year you will keep them within bounds and avoid the need for more drastic action. Shrubs such as broom, tamarisk and genista can have up to half of their new growth removed, while evergreen ceanothus, halimium, indigofera and cistus can have all flowered shoots cut back by up to two-thirds.

Routine pruning

Other spring- and early-summer-flowering deciduous shrubs do respond to being pruned back during early summer by producing new shoots lower down the pruned stem. The exact timing of the pruning will depend on the plant, the season and your local climate. All these shrubs flower on shoots produced during the previous season. So if you prune in spring you would lose the blooms for that year. Ideally, you should prune directly after the shrub has flowered. Your aim should not be to give an overall trim, but to make strategic cuts that will maintain the shrub's natural shape. After removing dead, diseased and damaged wood, thin overcrowded growth and then concentrate on wood that has produced flowers this year. As a rule, cut back each flowered stem by between a half and two-thirds, cutting just above a new shoot that will develop into next year's flowering stem.

Renovating old shrubs

Older shrubs may need more drastic pruning to reinvigorate them. For example, popular plants such as buddleias, kolkwitzia and flowering

SUMMER PRUNING SHRUBS

1 Philadelphus (illustrated) and some spring-flowering species, such as *Spiraea* 'Arguta' and *S. thunbergii*, become too dense and overcrowded if they are not pruned. Annual pruning keeps them compact and flowering well, and the best time to do this is immediately after flowering.

2 Reduce the shoots by one-third, cutting out the oldest and woodiest ones. Cut back the old stems to where a new shoot is growing lower down. Alternatively, if the shoot is very old and the bush is very congested, cut to just above the ground.

3 Brooms and genistas tend to become woody at the base as they age, with the flowers too high up the plants to look attractive. Keep them compact by regular pruning. Cut them back as soon as the flowers die and the seed pods are beginning to form.

The tender early-summer-flowering evergreen New Zealand tea tree (*Leptospermum scoparium* 'Lyndon') should be trimmed lightly after flowering to keep the shrub compact and tidy.

spiraeas can be pruned by removing one stem in three. Always choose the oldest and thickest stems to prune out so that the shrub will remain fresh, vigorous and free flowering.

Cultivars of lilac (*Syringa vulgaris*) often become tall and leggy, with the flowers borne very high up. You may be able to rejuvenate a neglected plant by sawing it down to a height of

30–90cm (1–3ft). This may sound drastic, and it will not flower for a year or two, but it should eventually shoot from the old wood and produce an attractive compact plant again.

4 Cut back each shoot to about halfway along the new green growth. Do not cut into old, woody growth because new shoots will be reluctant to sprout. Always cut back so that there are green shoots left on the plant to grow after pruning.

5 Lilacs benefit from careful deadheading. As soon as the flowering is over, cut the dead blooms back to the first pair of leaves below the flowerhead (no further, otherwise you might remove buds from which new flowering shoots will be produced).

No-prune shrubs

Abelia	*Elaeagnus*
Acer	*Euonymus*
palmatum	*fortunei*
Aucuba	*Fatsia japonica*
japonica	*Genista lydia*
Berberis	*Hamamelis*
thunbergii	*Ilex*
Choisya ternata	*Magnolia*
Cordyline	*stellata*
australis	*Pieris japonica*
Cotoneaster	*Prunus*
microphyllus	*laurocerasus*
Daphne	*Sarcococca*

Creating patio displays

Watering patio containers can be one of the most time-consuming tasks in the garden during the summer months. The more baskets, pots and tubs you have, the longer it takes, but you can reduce the workload by conserving the water applied as much as possible. Choosing the right sort of containers, compost and plants can minimize the amount of water required, and adopting a labour-saving watering regime will save time.

Choosing containers

Porous pots such as those made from plain terracotta lose water via evaporation through their sides.

Wooden containers, such as authentic Versailles pots and mock half-barrels, also leak water. Existing containers can be lined with plastic sheeting before planting to reduce water loss (take care not to cover the drainage holes), or if you are buying new choose non-porous plastic or glazed pots instead. You can also buy containers with built-in water reservoirs that will supply the plants with water automatically between waterings. It's also a good idea to choose the largest containers and hanging baskets you can afford, because these will hold a lot more compost (soil mix) and so require watering less frequently.

Choosing the right compost

Soil-based composts retain moisture better than soil-less or peat-based mixes, which are difficult to rewet if they dry out. Incorporate water-retaining granules in the compost before you plant or use a specially formulated container compost that already includes additional water-absorbing material. You can add water-retaining gel to existing pots by poking holes into the compost with a stick and trickling dry granules into each hole. Cover the tops of the holes with compost and then stand the pot in a bowl of water until thoroughly soaked.

Low-maintenance plants

You can reduce the need for watering by choosing plants that can tolerate drought. Sun-loving flowers such as gazanias, osteospermums and pelargoniums, grey-leaved plants such as *Convolvulus cneorum* and *Helichrysum petiolare*, and architectural plants such as agave, phormium and yucca, are all good choices.

Watering systems

For just one or two pots it is best to use a watering can. A few more can be tackled with a hose fitted with a trigger spray at the end. Long-reach

PLANTING A WINDOW BOX

1 Window boxes and troughs can be planted in the same way, but include more trailers in a window box than you would in a trough. Cover the drainage holes with a drainage layer of broken pots or gravel.

2 Half-fill the box or trough with compost (soil mix). A loam-based formula is suitable for troughs, but if the window box is to be fixed on brackets choose a lightweight mixture based on peat or a peat substitute.

3 Most people prefer a mixed planting, with some trailers and both flowering and foliage plants. To help you visualize how they will look, try arranging the plants while they are still in their pots before actually planting.

4 When the positions look right, insert the plants, firming the compost around each root-ball. Plant more closely than in beds or borders, and do not include plants that will overpower their neighbours.

5 Fill any gaps with compost and firm to remove air pockets. Water thoroughly after planting and make sure that the compost never dries out. In warm weather this may mean watering daily, or even more often.

versions are useful for watering hanging baskets and wall pots. If you have a large number of containers around the garden you might want to consider an automatic system that does the job for you. A micro-irrigation system is easy to install and consists of a series of micro-bore pipes that carry water from the main feeder pipe to individual nozzles positioned next to the plants. Adjustable nozzles are particularly useful because you can give each plant exactly the correct amount of water. The systems can be made completely automatic by plumbing them into the mains. You can fit a timer or even use a computer to regulate when and how much water is applied.

Creating better displays

Frost-tender bedding plants can now be planted out in all but the coldest areas, but be guided by your local conditions. Tubs and troughs packed with summer bedding plants are a sure-fire way to bring pockets of colour to less interesting parts of the garden. Make the most of window boxes, too, which will brighten the exterior of any home. Most people plant mixed groups, but sometimes a single-subject planting can look especially striking.

Because a window box is likely to be the first thing visitors see, make sure it is filled with long-lasting colour. Petunias and *Convolvulus sabatius* have been used here.

PLANTING UP TUBS AND PATIO POTS

1 Filled tubs and pots can be very heavy to move, so plant them up where they are to be displayed. Cover the drainage holes with a layer of broken pots, gravel or chipped bark.

2 A loam-based compost (soil mix) is best for most plants, but if the pot is to be used where weight is a consideration, such as on a balcony, use a soil-less mixture.

3 Choose a tall or bold plant for the centre, such as *Cordyline australis* or a fuchsia, or one with large flowers, such as the osteospermum that has been used here. This will provide a focal point for the scheme.

4 Fill in around the edge with some bushier but lower growing plants. Mixing several types can create a riotus, colourful display; for a more formal effect, you could choose just one variety for the edge.

5 Water thoroughly after planting and cover the surface with a decorative mulch, such as chipped bark or cocoa shells, if much of the surface is visible (this is worth doing anyway to conserve moisture).

Propagating shrubs and climbers

Many species of shrub and climber are easy to propagate at this time of the year. Raising your own plants from scratch not only provides a great deal of satisfaction but will save a lot of money too. If, for example, you are planning a new hedge, border edging or want to fill a new shrubbery with specimens and groundcover, you can do it for next to nothing by propagating the plants yourself.

Why take cuttings?

Several of the most popular edging plants are easy to root from cuttings. If you want to frame a border with santolina or create a French-style potager with box edging, take cuttings now. Small-leaved hebes

If you want an easy-care groundcover for a sunny spot, rock roses (*Helianthemum*) are easy to propagate from cuttings taken in summer.

TAKING SEMI-RIPE CUTTINGS

1 Choose shoots that are almost fully grown except for the soft tip. The base of the cutting should be hardening, even though the tip may still be soft. Most cuttings are best made from pieces 5–10cm (2–4in) long.

2 Trim the bottom of the cutting just below a leaf joint, then strip the lower leaves from each cutting to leave a short length of clear stem to insert into the soil. Do not damage the stem as you remove unwanted leaves.

3 The use of a rooting compound is optional. Dip the cut end into the powder, liquid or gel, but if using a powder dip the very ends into water first so that the powder adheres. Shake or gently tap off any excess.

4 Cuttings taken from hardy plants will root outside at this time of year, though they will perform better in a coldframe or propagator.

5 Firm the soil around the cuttings to make sure there are no large pockets of air, which might cause the new roots to dry out.

6 Remember to insert a label. This is especially important if you are rooting a number of different kinds of shrubs.

and dwarf forms of lavender can also be propagated in this way and will be ideal additions to informal as well as formal garden designs. Useful groundcover plants, such as *Euonymus fortunei* 'Emerald 'n' Gold' and periwinkles, are very easy to root from cuttings, as are ivies and the beautiful sprawling summer-flowering helianthemum.

Even if you are not planning major improvements to your garden, there are other good reasons to propagate some plants now. For example, if you have one or two borderline hardy shrubs, such as abelia, cistus or escallonia, it would make sense to take cuttings now as an insurance against winter losses – especially if you live in a colder area or if your garden is exposed. The rooted cuttings would be easy to keep protected in an insulated coldframe or unheated greenhouse, porch or conservatory. Similarly, if you plan to move a mature shrub this autumn you can insure against its loss by taking cuttings now. A few shrubs are rather short lived or get straggly with age, so need to be replaced on a regular basis. By taking cuttings in summer you can have

Some shrubs to propagate from semi-ripe cuttings

Berberis	Hebe
Buddleja	Helianthemum
Camellia	Hydrangea
Ceanothus	Ilex
Choisya	Indigofera
Cistus	Kolkwitzia
Cotoneaster	Lavatera
Daphne	Ligustrum
cneorum	Philadelphus
Escallonia	Phlomis
Fatsia Japonica	Potentilla
Forsythia	Pyracantha
Fuchsia	Rosmarinus
Griselinia	Weigela

LAYERING SHRUBS

1 Find a low-growing shoot that can be easily pegged down to the ground. Trim off the leaves only from the area that will be in direct contact with the soil.

2 Bend the stem down until it touches the ground. Make a hole 10cm (4in) deep, with the side nearer to the parent plant sloping but the other side vertical.

3 Slit the stem on the underside to injure it. Peg it into the hole with a piece of bent wire or a peg, using the vertical face of the excavation to keep the shoot upright.

4 Return the soil and firm it well. If you keep the ground moist, roots should form and within 12–18 months you should be able to sever the new plant from its parent.

replacements ready when they need replacing. Jerusalem sage and shrubby potentillas both fall into this category.

Semi-ripe cuttings

Take semi-ripe or summer cuttings any time between midsummer and early autumn. By this time of year the new shoots will have started to turn brown and woody at the base, but will still be pliable. There are four main types of cuttings: basal, trimmed at the point it joined the woody stem on the parent plant; nodal, trimmed just below a leaf joint (node); internodal, trimmed halfway between two leaf joints; and heel, pulled from the parent plant with a little bark from the woody

stem to which it was attached. Which type you choose should depend on the plant and its type of growth. Dip the cutting in a fungicidal solution to guard against rotting off, or in a hormone rooting compound (which usually also contains a fungicide). Insert in a pot covered in a plastic bag if you are rooting just a few cuttings, or use a coldframe for large batches. Keep the cuttings cool and shaded from direct sunlight.

Layering shrubs

This technique is usually used for shrubby plants with low branches that can be easily pegged to the ground, but a few border plants can also be layered – carnations and pinks are often raised this way.

Propagating flowers and bulbs

You can raise many popular flowers from seed saved from the garden, while others are easy to propagate by division, layering and cuttings. Collecting seed from annual flowers is particularly worthwhile because this means you won't have to buy fresh for next year. The seed from many perennials is also worth collecting, especially if you want to raise a lot of plants for a new border. If you are planning to move house, collecting seed is an easy way of taking many of your favourite flowers with you without destroying the existing display.

Saving your own seed

Although most flowers can be raised from collected seed, it is worth bearing in mind that not all will produce plants that are identical to the parent plant. For example, highly bred hybrids (such as F1s and F2s) do not come true from seed, while many plants with variegated foliage tend to produce seedlings with plain-green leaves. However, it may be worth using collected seed, since the natural variation may lead to interesting new varieties as well as some inevitable disappointments.

SAVING FLOWER SEED

1 Cut the seedhead from the plant when it ripens. If the plant has explosive seedheads, cover with a paper bag before the flowerhead is fully ripe to catch the seed as it is ejected.

2 Seed can be collected from seedpods by tapping the seedhead over a sheet of white paper. Remove any debris and pour the seed into a labelled envelope.

Propagating bulbs and rhizomes

Rhizomatous irises – that is, all irises except for the spring-flowering bulbous types – can be propagated after flowering but before the end of autumn. The rhizomes are really fleshy, creeping stems. Over time, they form congested clumps on the surface of the soil. Lift the clumps, trim the leaves and use a sharp knife to cut off the young, fresh rhizomes around the edge of the clump. Discard the old, woody sections. Replant the trimmed sections, making sure that each new piece has

several healthy leaves, into the weeded and ready ground.

When the flowers have died down, lily bulbs can be propagated by separating and growing on the bulbils that develop in the leaf axils of some species. The outer scales on the bulbs of some types of lily can be encouraged to form new bulbs by being kept in a moist growing medium, although this is a slow process.

Some plants, such as hardy geraniums, spread their seed using explosive seedheads. These should be carefully bagged on the plant before they are ripe, otherwise they will scatter the seed as you are trying to collect it. Use a paper bag, never plastic, which will encourage moulds. A paper bag is ideal for collecting non-explosive seedheads too. In this case, cut them off the plant and place in labelled bags in a box. Large flowerheads in seed can either be cut from the plant and placed in the paper bag or laid on a sheet of white paper in a seed tray to collect the seed. Hang up the bags in a warm, dry, airy place where the seeds can be allowed to ripen fully without being disturbed – an airing cupboard would be ideal.

DIVIDING FLAG IRISES

1 If the rhizomes of flag irises have become very congested, lift the clump with a fork and cut away and discard the oldest parts. Use only the current season's growth for replanting.

2 Trim the leaves to stumps about 5–8cm (2–3in) long. Replant the pieces of rhizome on a slight ridge of soil, covering the roots but leaving the tops exposed.

It is easy to propagate lilies, such as the popular Turkscap lily (*Lilium martagon*), to create a spectacular summer display. The bulbs can be divided once the flowers and foliage have died down.

Clean the seed before storing by shaking them out of their seedpods and removing any bits of seed capsule and other debris. The easiest way to do this with large seed is to pick out the seed individually by hand. Smaller seed can be sieved. Place the clean seed into labelled paper

envelopes and store in an airtight container with a packet of silica gel to absorb any moisture. Some perennial flowers need special seed treatments, such as a period of cold, before they will germinate, so check this in a good plant encyclopaedia before you sow and take action if necessary.

Layering carnations

Border carnations and pinks root quickly from layers prepared now. Select a few well-spaced, non-flowering shoots, remove all but the top four leaves. Slit each one below the lowest pair of leaves, and peg the shoot – slit down – into good soil.

PROPAGATING LILIES

1 Take a clean, dormant bulb and snap off some outer scales, as close to the base as possible. Be careful not to damage the scales as you remove them from the bulb.

2 Put the scales in a bag of fungicide and gently shake to coat them. Prepare a mixture of equal parts peat (or an alternative) and perlite or vermiculite in a plastic bag.

3 Dampen the mix. Shake the scales free of excess fungicide and place them in the bag. Store in a warm, dark place for 6–8 weeks and plant up when bulblets appear.

Maintaining the pond

If it has been well sited, constructed and stocked, a pond will require a minimum of attention during the summer months apart from the occasional topping up after a hot spell to maintain water levels and help prevent water temperatures fluctuating too much. Small ponds and water features, such as gurgle ponds, that do not have a large reservoir of water may need topping up every day if they are operated during hot weather.

Protect fish

If you see the fish gulping for air at the surface during close, thundery weather it's worth playing a hosepipe on to the water surface to help increase oxygen levels. If the pond is fitted with a fountain or other moving water feature, turn this on to achieve the same result. The water temperature of shallow ponds that are stocked with fish may increase too much in prolonged hot spells, endangering the survival of the fish. If your fish look distressed, transfer them to a tank somewhere cool and shady until conditions improve.

Fish may also be at risk from predators outside the pond. If herons sometimes visit your garden, it is worth netting the pond in summer or putting up a low wire fence about 45cm (18in) high to

Introduce tender plants

Summer is the ideal time to add exotic-looking, tender aquatic plants, such as water hyacinths and water lettuce. Water chestnuts are the exception to this rule since although the plants are killed in winter, they produce 'nuts' that sink to the bottom of the pond in autumn and sprout the following spring to grow into new plants.

put them off preying on your fish.

Feed fish throughout the summer months as required, taking care not to overfeed them as surplus food will sink and rot in the water.

CLEARING POND WEEDS

1 Left untreated, the filaments of blanketweed will quickly take over a pond. To clear the water, insert a cane into the water and twist it to wind the weed around it, rather like candyfloss.

2 Numerous tiny creatures live in blanketweed, and the removed weed should be left at the side of the pond for a while so that the creatures can escape and return to the water. Then put it on the compost heap.

3 Oxygenating and floating plants can soon take over small ponds. Lift out clumps and tear them apart, returning about a half to two-thirds to the water. Leave unwanted sections near the pond for a while.

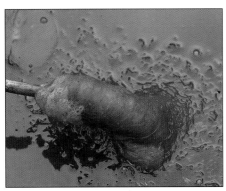

4 Duckweed or other floaters can be useful initially in preventing green water, but they soon spread and need constant thinning, otherwise they can prevent more desirable plants from growing well.

5 Remove duckweed using a fine-mesh net before it has a chance to spread. You will need to check for it on a regular basis because even a small colony can quickly spread in the right conditions.

6 Even a pond that is clear of pond weeds can become infested by small amounts being introduced on new plants. Always check new plants carefully, looking on the undersides of leaves to check they are clean.

Clear water

Hot summer weather can also upset the ecological balance of a pond so that the water turns green with algae. This can be controlled quickly and easily using a pond algicide, but make sure you follow the instructions carefully so that you don't affect other aquatic residents. If you do not want to use chemicals you can clear the surface by scooping out blanket weed by hand. Simply use a stick or bamboo cane to twist up the filamentous blanketweed algae into a green blob wrapped around the cane so that it can be removed from the pond. Leave the weed at the side of the pond overnight to allow any aquatic creatures to escape back into the pond before putting it on the compost heap. For a long-term solution, consider installing a filter, which will remove the algae before it has time to bloom. You can also prevent algae forming in the first place by placing a special barley-straw pad into the pond. It is thought that the bacteria found on it feed on the algae, keeping the water clear – even during hot spells.

If duckweed is a problem, use a fine-mesh net (the sort sold for

Thin overcrowded lily pads before they cover the entire surface of the pond.

WATER LEVEL

Top up the level of water in the pool in summer when evaporation levels are high. This is especially important if you have a watercourse running continuously.

rockpool fishing at the seaside) to scoop up the tiny floating plants. Leave the plants on the side of the pond for 24 hours so that any trapped creatures can escape.

Tidy plants

It's not too late to add new plants to your pond in midsummer, although you'll get maximum benefit if you plant up your pond earlier in the year. Existing repeat-flowering marginal plants will benefit from regular deadheading to tidy the displays and encourage further flushes of blooms. Remove rampant plants and thin them to prevent them from swamping their neighbours. Overcrowded waterlilies should also be thinned out so they do not cover the entire surface of the pond.

Use a garden hose to dislodge and drown pests, such as blackfly and thrips, which can form colonies on waterlily pads. Lush marginal plants such as marsh marigolds can suffer from mildew. Cut off affected leaves to encourage new, disease-free growth.

Planting and maintaining the flower garden

Spring-flowering bulbs are now becoming widely available, but exactly when you plant them will depend largely on whether the ground has been cleared of summer plants. If you are planting in beds, it is best to let the summer bedding continue to flower for as long as possible, and you may prefer not to disturb the last of the summer colour in herbaceous borders just yet, but it is best to plant as soon as possible in vacant ground and in containers. It is also worth spending time on late flowering chrysanthemums and dahlias to get the best displays possible.

Planting bulbs

If you have a lot of bulbs to plant over a wide area, individual planting holes may be more appropriate than excavating several large holes to take a group of bulbs. There are special long-handled planting tools that are useful for individual bulbs, but an ordinary long-handled trowel is just as good. You can use a normal trowel with a handle of conventional length, but it makes planting more tedious if the area is large. Check from time to time to make sure that the holes are being made to the correct depth. After checking a few it will be easy to judge by eye. Make a hole large

enough to take the bulb easily (it must not become wedged in the hole, because the roots will then be exposed to dry air and will not grow). Return the excavated soil. If you are planting a large area, you can shuffle it back in with your feet, then rake the surface level.

Planting depth

The depth and spacing of the bulbs should depend on the type of bulb you are planting. As a rule of thumb, a bulb should be covered with soil equivalent to twice its own depth. This means that a 5cm (2in) high bulb should be planted in a 15cm

PLANTING BULBS FOR SPRING

1 Fork over the ground before planting, and if the plants are to be left undisturbed for some years, add some well-rotted organic material. If your soil is heavy, most bulbs will also benefit from the addition of some sharp sand or grit.

2 Rake a slow-acting fertilizer, such as bonemeal, which contains mainly phosphate, into the surface, or apply it to the planting holes. Alternatively, apply a controlled-release fertilizer that provides nutrients according to the soil temperature in spring.

3 If you are planting a permanent display in a bed or border and have space, dig out a hole about three times the depth of the bulbs and wide enough to take the number of bulbs you wish to plant. Make the hole irregular for a more natural, informal effect.

4 Space the bulbs so that they look like a natural clump. Wide spacing will allow for future growth and natural increase, but if you intend to lift the bulbs after flowering much closer spacing will create a bolder display.

5 Set the bulbs on their base. Draw the soil back over the bulbs, being careful not to dislodge them in the process. Firm the soil with the back of the rake rather than treading it, which may damage the bulbs.

6 If you are likely to cultivate the area before the shoots come through, mark where bulbs have been planted and label. Alternatively, make a record in a notebook of where the bulbs have been planted for future reference.

CARING FOR DAHLIAS AND CHRYSANTHEMUMS

1 To produce larger flowers, pinch out the side buds behind the crown (central) flower bud of dahlias, while they are still small. Many chrysanthemums are also disbudded, but how and when you do it depends on the cultivar, so be guided by a specialist catalogue.

2 The best way to control pests and diseases is to spray at the first signs. Often it may be possible to prevent spread simply by pinching off and destroying the first few affected leaves. The discoloured chrysanthemum leaves show signs of leaf miner damage.

3 Chrysanthemums and dahlias benefit from regular feeding. Even if you used a slow-release fertilizer to see them through most of the summer, they will probably respond to a boost now. Apply a quick-acting general fertilizer or a high-potash formulation.

(6in) hole. Larger bulbs should be spaced 8–10cm (3–4in) apart, and smaller bulbs 2.5–5cm (1–2in) apart. If you are trying to create an instant natural-looking effect, plant the bulbs more densely than this. But if you are prepared to wait, plant at the standard distance and the bulbs will spread naturally. Some bulbs, such as daffodils, spread mainly by offshoots from the bulb so they form larger and larger clumps. Others, such as crocus, seed themselves more widely.

Most bulbs have an easily identifiable top and bottom, but some, and many corms and tubers, can cause confusion because they lack an obvious growing point. If in doubt, just plant them on their side – the shoot will grow upwards and the roots down. A few bulbs that do have an obvious top are planted on their side because the crown tends to rot in wet soil, though these are rare exceptions. *Fritillaria imperialis* is sometimes planted this way. It is also worth planting vulnerable bulbs on a bed of grit or coarse sand to allow good drainage around the base.

Dahlias and chrysanthemums

At the end of summer and into autumn, dahlias and chrysanthemums come into their true glory, just as most flowers have passed their best. Some types are simply left to produce masses of blooms with no intervention, but those grown for large flowers are usually selectively disbudded (see above). This produces fewer but larger blooms. Alternatively you can promote a mass of smaller flowers later by removing the terminal bud only. Both types of plant need plenty of feeding and a careful watch has to be kept to prevent pests and diseases spoiling them.

Disbud dahlias to get larger blooms on single stems that are suitable for the show bench and for use in arrangements.

Maintaining shrubs and hedges

Permanent feature plants, such as hedges and groundcover, need to be attended to at this time of the year. A hedge that has been allowed to grow out of control or one that has bare patches can be an eyesore. This is the time to carry out the essential maintenance that will prepare such features for winter and keep them looking good next year.

Trimming a hedge

Hedges need regular trimming to promote dense bushy growth from the base to the top. Most formal hedges are best trimmed in late summer with a pair of shears or a powered hedgetrimmer. Large-leaved hedges should be cut with secateurs (pruners) so that you avoid cutting through individual leaves, which could look unsightly. Slow-growing hedging plants, such as yew, holly and beech, need trimming only once a year, but faster-growing hedges, such as privet and box-leaved honeysuckle (*Lonicera nitida*), will require trimming regularly from late spring. Informal hedges also need pruning to keep them in shape. If it is a flowering hedge or one that bears a crop of decorative berries you will need to prune at the right time. For example, berberis, escallonia and *Ribes sanguineum* should be trimmed immediately after flowering, if necessary.

It is important to shape an established hedge so that it grows well and remains healthy. The easiest shape for most formal hedges is to create a square-sided profile with a domed or slightly sloping top. Use a coloured line held taut between canes at either end of the hedge as a guide. If you live in an area that regularly gets heavy snowfalls in winter, it is important to create a smoothly domed top so that the snow is shed naturally and doesn't accumulate on the top and push the hedge out of shape. You can either shape the top by eye or cut a template out of wood

KEEPING HEDGES IN TRIM

1 Cutting a hedge also includes clearing up the trimmings afterwards. One way of making this task a little less onerous is to lay down a cloth or plastic sheet under the area you are clipping and to move it along as you go.

2 When you are using shears, try to keep the blades flat against the plane of the hedge because this will give an even cut. If you jab the shears forward with a stabbing motion, the result is likely to be uneven.

3 A formal hedge looks best if the top is kept accurately level. This can be done by inserting poles at the ends or spaced at intervals along the hedge, with strings stretched between them to use as a guide.

4 Keep the blades flat when you cut the top of a hedge. If it is a tall hedge, you will need to use steps or a platform rather than reaching up at an angle. Make sure any support is held very stable.

5 Power trimmers are much faster than hand shears and, in consequence, things can go wrong faster as well, so concentrate on what you are doing and have a rest if your arms feel tired. Wear adequate protective gear.

6 Some conifers are relatively slow growing and produce only a few stray stems that can be cut off with secateurs (pruners) to neaten them. Secateurs should also be used for large-leaved shrubs, such as laurel.

TRIMMING GROUNDCOVER

1 Groundcover is often neglected and tends to collect all kinds of litter and rubbish. Take time to regularly remove any litter that is lurking between the leaves.

2 Most groundcover will look better if it is trimmed back at least once a year. Here, a lesser periwinkle (*Vinca minor*) is given a much-needed trim.

3 Regular trimming will encourage groundcover plants to grow more densely, with fewer straggly stems. They will look tidier and healthier.

to use as a guide. Hedges with very dense growth, such as yew and most other conifers, should not be cut with vertical sides, but trimmed in a tapering wedge shape that is wider at the base than at the top. This shape allows the base of the hedge to get plenty of light so that it will be more likely to remain densely clothed in foliage. Before you cut, you can spread plastic sheeting along the hedge to make it easier to clear up the clippings afterwards.

REVERSION IN SHRUBS

Green-leaved shoots have appeared in this *Spiraea japonica* 'Goldflame'. If left, they will take over the whole plant because they are more vigorous. The remedy is simple. Cut the offending shoots back to that part of the stem or shoot where the reversion begins.

When to trim hedges?

Evergreen hedges	Growth rate	When to trim
Buxus sempervirens	Slow	Midsummer
Chamaecyparis lawsoniana	Fast	Early summer and late summer
x *Cupressocyparis leylandii*	Very fast	Early summer
Euonymus japonicus	Slow	Late summer
Griselinia littoralis	Medium	Late summer
Ilex aquifolium	Slow	Late summer
Ligustrum ovalifolium	Fast	Late spring to late summer
Lonicera nitida	Fast	Late spring to late summer
Prunus lusitanica	Slow	Late summer
Taxus baccata	Slow	Late summer
Thuja plicata	Medium	Late summer

Deciduous hedges		
Carpinus betulus	Medium	Late summer
Fagus sylvatica	Slow	Late summer
Prunus cerasifera	Medium	Late summer

Flowering hedges		
Berberis darwinii	Medium	After flowering
Berberis x *stenophylla*	Medium	After flowering
Berberis thunbergii	Medium	After flowering
Crataegus monogyna	Medium	Late winter
Escallonia cultivars	Medium	After flowering
Fuchsia magellanica	Fast	Mid-spring
Garrya elliptica	Medium	After flowering
Ribes sanguineum	Medium	After flowering
Rosa	Medium	Early spring

Autumn

Autumn can be an Indian summer or the first taste of winter, so you will need to keep a close eye on weather forecasts. Normally the shortening days and lower sun will mean temperatures slowly decrease as the season progresses. Misty mornings and dewy evenings become commonplace, creating an eerie atmosphere in the lower light levels. Be watchful and vigilant as the nights become colder. In some areas quite severe frosts are common in early autumn, and in others light frosts may not occur until mid- or late autumn, if at all. Listen to the weather forecasts and take in or protect vulnerable plants if frost is expected. Think seriously about winter protection for plants on the borderline of hardiness, and be prepared to give early winter shelter, perhaps in the form of a windbreak, for newly planted evergreens. A little protection can ensure that many plants survive instead of succumbing to winter winds and cold.

Japanese maples are one of the best small trees for autumn colour, with leaves turning brilliant shades of yellow, red and orange.

The Autumn Garden

The weather in early autumn is still warm enough to make outdoor gardening a comfortable experience, and although the vibrant flowers of summer may be gone, there are plenty of delights to be enjoyed in the form of bright berries and flaming foliage, not to mention late-flowering gems such as chrysanthemums and asters. Apart from bulb planting, and protecting frost-tender plants, there are few really pressing jobs at this time of year.

Early Autumn

Once the grass has stopped growing, the lawn may be given its final cut – the timing will vary depending on the weather and where you live. It is therefore an ideal time to clean and service your lawnmower. Early autumn is also the perfect time to complete lawn maintenance tasks such as raking out thatch, eradicating moss, feeding and aerating, to improve the quality of your lawn.

Make the most of autumn leaves by collecting them up promptly and composting them. It is a good idea to clear leaves from your lawn and other low-growing plants regularly to prevent them being smothered and suffering stress before the onset of winter.

There's still time to plant most spring-flowering bulbs in the garden or containers. Daffodils, crocuses and other popular bulbs should be planted as soon as possible, otherwise flowering may be delayed the following spring. Tulips are the exception: they should be planted in late autumn to reduce the possiblity of disease.

In the greenhouse, you can extend the season by removing any shading materials and cleaning the outside of the greenhouse to enhance light levels as much as possible. There's still time to sow a few annuals and perennials destined for the garden.

Chrysanthemums provide some welcome warmth of colour as the days grow cooler into the autumn.

Fuchsias flower from summer until the first frosts. They can look fantastic in beds and borders, as wall shrubs, and in containers and hanging baskets.

Mid-autumn

This is an unpredictable time of the year. In cold regions quite severe frosts are not uncommon, while in mild climates some plants are still growing and tender plants may survive for another month or more. This is a time to be on the alert for frost warnings if you haven't yet had the first frost. Be flexible and garden with an eye to the weather as well as the calendar.

You can transform the outlook from your house by planting containers for a winter display. Make the most of winter-flowering plants, evergreens, ornamental cabbages and plants with decorative winter berries.

Mid-autumn is an ideal time to plant trees, shrubs and hardy perennials. Although container-grown specimens can be planted at any time when the soil is not too wet or frozen, autumn is best in many ways since the soil is usually moist and still warm enough to promote quick establishment.

Extreme cold and wet are the two main winter killers in the garden. You can take steps now to protect your plants by putting up barriers, insulating containers, wrapping top growth and keeping off the rain. It's also the time to prepare your greenhouse for winter if you intend to continue to use it during the coldest months. Check the heater is in good working order well before it is needed and put up greenhouse insulation to cut down on heating costs.

Trees and shrubs that take on autumnal lives, such as this cut-leaf maple, provide some extra colour at this time of year.

Late Autumn

A last-minute spurt of action is often needed at this time of year, to get the garden ready for winter and ensure protection for plants that need it. In cold areas winter will already have taken its grip, but in warmer climates there are still many mild days to be enjoyed. Take advantage of them before colder temperatures and strong winds drive you indoors.

It is also important to keep on top of other routine tasks if the weather is mild. There will be plenty of weeding to be done, especially in mild spells, since weeds seem to keep growing more vigorously than other plants – they may begin colonizing spaces where flowers have died down. You should also carry on clearing fallen leaves from around the garden. If left, the leaves will provide a haven for slugs and other pests.

A mild spell in late autumn is an ideal time to clean the greenhouse. It is likely to be less full than in spring, and it is important to start the season of cold, dull days with clean glass to allow in all available light, and an environment as free as possible of pests and diseases. Any outdoor plants that are likely to be damaged by winter weather can be protected now. Evergreens such as conifers may need protection from strong winds, especially when newly planted. Alpines and some other plants are more susceptible to damage from rain, though the low temperatures will not harm them – these can be sheltered by a glass 'roof'.

Late autumn is an ideal time to plant deciduous trees. The secret to success when planting is to prepare the ground well and plant firmly so the roots cannot move.

The ice plant (*Sedum spectabile*) tolerates drought and flowers late. It is therefore ideal for brightening the garden in the early autumn.

Planting spring and summer flowers

If frosts have not put an abrupt end to your summer bedding display, the plants will undoubtedly be looking sad and dejected by now. Even if you do not plan to replant with spring bedding, the garden will look tidier if the old plants are cleared away and the ground dug over. If they are not diseased, most can go straight on the compost heap, but this is a good time to harvest some ripe seed for sowing next year, or straight away if the plants are hardy enough.

Gladioli can be left in the ground only in mild areas where the soil is well drained. If your soil does not remain wet, and if frosts are always light and do not penetrate far into the soil, they should survive. In cold areas, however, gladioli will be killed if they remain in the soil, so lift them before there are penetrating frosts. Gladioli flower reliably from year to year, so they are almost always worth saving. The offsets or cormlets (small corms) that form around the base will reach flowering size within two or three years if they are potted up and kept in frost-free conditions until spring. Cormlets may not come true to type, however.

If you have a well-drained, sunny border, plant bulbs like agapanthus and lilies now for a spectacular display next summer.

Plant spring displays

Fork over the ground after clearing it of summer bedding plants. Fertilizer is not normally needed, but bonemeal, which is very slow-acting, or another slow-release product, is worth adding if the soil is impoverished. Bulbs should be planted as soon after purchase as possible. If you have raised spring bedding plants yourself, water them well about an hour before lifting them with as much soil around the roots as possible. Plants, such as forget-me-nots and double daisies, bought from garden centres are usually sold in trays or strips. Don't be afraid to break them if this allows you to release the rootball with as little root disturbance as possible. Space the plants out on the surface, allowing for the bulbs, before planting. Space the bulbs out, then begin planting from the back or one end.

CLEARING SUMMER BEDDING

1 Plants like this will do more good on the compost heap than they will left on show. Bare soil can look neat and tidy as long as you remove weeds and other debris.

2 Bedding plants generally have shallow roots and are easy to pull up by hand. If some have deep roots, simply loosen the roots with a hand fork before you start.

3 Old bedding plants, as long as they are not diseased, are ideal for the compost heap. You can collect them all together before filling your compost bin.

Plant lilies for summer

Lilies are often planted in spring, but you can also plant them now except in very cold areas. The bulbs are less likely to dry out, which can result in failures. Most lilies prefer a slightly acid soil (pH 6–6.5), but some, including *Lilium candidum*, will do well in alkaline soils. Lilies demand a well-prepared site, so dig the soil deeply and work in as much well-rotted manure or garden compost as you can spare. Add plenty of grit to improve drainage if the soil tends to be wet. Lilies look best in groups rather than as isolated specimens, so excavate an area of soil to a depth of about 20cm (8in), large enough to take at least four or five bulbs. Add coarse grit or sand unless the soil is very well drained. Add a sprinkling of bonemeal or a slow-release fertilizer, because initial feeding is more important than with bedding bulbs used for a single season. Space the bulbs about 15cm (6in) apart and make sure that they are deep enough to be covered with about twice their own depth of soil. Sprinkle more grit or coarse sand around the bulbs to deter slugs and reduce the risk of waterlogging. Place small canes or sticks around the

planting area before you return the soil to remind you to avoid damaging the emerging shoots when you hoe in spring. Remember to label.

1 Loosen the soil with a spade or fork before attempting to lift the plants.

2 Trim off most of the foliage, leaving just a stub to dry off. Shake off most of the soil.

3 Leave the lifted plants in a dry, well-ventilated place for a few days to dry off. When the remains of the old stems have shrivelled, trim them off and remove the cormlets that have grown around the base.

4 Dust with fungicide by shaking in a bag containing a little fungicide. Then store the corms in paper bags in a dry and cool but frost-free place. Label clearly. Pot up the cormlets and keep frost-free.

Storing garden canes

Bamboo canes deteriorate after a season or two in use, especially if they have been left in the ground for a long period. Extend their life by cleaning and preserving them. Store them in a dry place rather than leaving them exposed in the garden. Knock off most of the soil, then scrub the canes with a stiff brush and garden or household disinfectant. Stand the ends that have been in the soil in a bucket or container partly filled with a wood preservative and leave overnight to allow the preservative to penetrate. Bind the cracked ends of canes with tape. Bundle the canes to keep them tidy and store in a dry place until needed next year.

4 Dig over the ground and remove any perennial weeds. If there are a lot of annual weeds, you can bury them by turning the soil with a spade, otherwise use a fork.

5 Whether or not you are replanting with spring bedding, rake the ground so that it is neat and tidy. On heavy soils, leave clods on the surface to be broken down by frost.

Preparing the lawn for winter

The time consuming task of mowing will now be coming to an end, but there are other tasks that can usefully be done now to keep your lawn in good condition. Clearing fallen leaves is essential, otherwise the grass will turn yellow, and if moss is a problem, you can take steps to eradicate it now. Moss-killing chemicals are only a temporary solution, however – to discourage moss, improve drainage by aerating the lawn, and feed as necessary to keep the grass growing strongly.

Removing thatch and moss

If moss is a problem in your lawn, treat with a moss-killer and allow it to turn brown before raking or scarifying (otherwise you'll just spread the moss around the lawn). Raking out thatch and moss from your lawn by hand is tiring. If you have a large lawn, you may wish to invest in a powered lawn rake. This will do the job rapidly and efficiently.

Spiking

If part of your lawn is used as a short cut or has been compacted through constant use, from summer games for example, you can improve

COLLECTING AND COMPOSTING LEAVES

1 Don't let leaves lie on your lawn. The grass beneath will turn yellow and be prone to disease and the leaves will harbour pests. On a small lawn, rake them up with a lawn rake.

3 You can buy special tools to lift the leaves without too much bending, but two pieces of wood are also an effective way to lift them once they have been brushed into a heap.

2 Leaves on paths and drives are best brushed up with a broom or besom. Alternatively, buy or hire a garden vacuum that will clear leaves from all parts of the garden.

4 Leaves can be added to the compost heap or bin, but some rot down slowly, so it is best to compost a large amount on their own. Leaf mould is a valuable soil improver.

it now by aerating it. Spike small areas with a garden fork pushed at least 10–15cm (4–6in) into the ground, spacing the holes a few

centimetres/inches apart. Wiggle the fork backwards and forwards each time to open up the holes. Take the drudgery out of aerating large areas

MAINTAINING THE LAWN

1 Over the years, grass clippings, dead grass and other debris form a thatch on the surface of your lawn. This affects growth of the grass and should be removed with a lawn rake. Raking also removes moss.

2 If grass growth is poor, aerate the lawn. You can do this by pushing the prongs of a garden fork into the ground to a depth of at least 15cm (6in), covering the entire area with holes that are no more than 10cm (4in) apart.

3 Brush a soil improver into the holes. Use lawn sand or a mixture of fine soil and sand if the ground is poorly drained. Alternatively, use peat, a peat substitute or sifted, well-rotted compost if the ground is already sandy.

by using a hollow-tined aerator that removes a core of soil efficiently. Then brush a 50:50 mixture of sifted garden soil and sharp sand (or just sharp sand on poorly drained lawns) into the holes. This will improve the drainage and aeration in the surface layer of the lawn.

Feeding

Most lawns don't require feeding in autumn, but if yours has seen excessive wear and tear during the summer months you might want to give it a boost now. Don't be tempted to use a spring lawn feed because this contains too much nitrogen. Nitrogen encourages lush, leafy growth that will be easily damaged by frost and is prone to diseases. Instead, choose a proprietary autumn lawn feed that will promote good root growth and tough topgrowth.

Weeding

Single weeds can be removed with an old kitchen knife or a spot weedkiller. Make sure you remove the tap root as well as the top growth when you remove each weed. If the weeds are more widespread, a combined weed and autumn feed product should be applied.

Routinely clear fallen leaves from around deciduous trees, like this cut-leaf maple, each autumn to prevent them from smothering low-growing plants and grass.

Collecting leaves

Never waste the leaves shed by deciduous trees and shrubs. They will make excellent leafmould if you rot them down, but if left on the ground, they can damage areas of grass and smother small plants. For small quantities, fill punctured black plastic sacks with moist leaves and tie the top to seal them in. Tuck the bags out of the way and the leaves will rot down. For crumbly leafmould suitable for use as a soil improver or planting mixture for next spring, mix a few handfuls of grass clippings in with each sack. For large quantities, make a special cage by driving four strong posts into the ground and wrapping chicken wire around them. Fill with leaves. If the leaves are dry, sprinkle them with water and cover the top with a piece of carpet to weigh them down and encourage decomposition.

4 If your lawn is in poor condition and needs reviving, apply an autumn lawn feed. It is essential that you use one that is specially formulated for autumn use, as spring and summer feeds will contain too much nitrogen.

5 If the grass contains a lot of moss, apply a moss-killer recommended for autumn use. The mixture known as lawn sand, sometimes used to kill moss, contains too much nitrogen and will encourage sappy growth.

Wildflower meadows

Autumn is the ideal time to tidy up wildflower meadows that contain summer-flowering plants. Once the wildflowers have set seed, use a scythe to cut the meadow back. For larger areas, hire a powered mechanical version.

Leave the cut material to dry so that any seed has time to ripen and scatter before the trimmings are gathered up and placed in a compost bin for recycling.

Repairing lawns

Threadbare lawns are a common sight at this time of the year after a summer's wear and tear. The stresses caused by drought are compounded by constant use and abuse during the summer months. Fortunately, early autumn is an ideal time to deal with many lawn problems. Any repairs made now will have time to bed in over winter while the grass is not being cut to ensure a fresh green lawn next spring. Now is also the perfect time to make a new lawn, by sowing seed or laying turf.

Humps and hollows

Uneven patches can appear on any lawn at any time, and are usually first detected when pale and dark green patches are seen after the lawn has been cut. Where there are humps, the grass is cut short and often scalped by the passing lawnmower blades, while grass in the dips remains long.

If the problem is widespread, then the best solution for dealing with hollows is to spike the lawn with a garden fork after it has been cut, then add a topdressing of finely

REPAIRING A BROKEN EDGE

1 Use a half-moon edging tool or a spade to cut a rectangle around the affected area, making sure that you cut back to firm soil.

2 Push a spade under the rectangle, starting from the broken edge. Keep the thickness of the slice of grass as even as possible.

3 Reverse the turf so that the undamaged part of the turf is against the edge of the bed and the broken edge is within the lawn. Fill the hole created by the damaged area with sifted soil and firm it down well.

4 Sow grass seed in the patched area, matching the type of grass if possible. Brush soil into the joints to help the grass knit together quickly and water well. Protect the newly-sown area from birds.

sieved topsoil, which should be spread out evenly. Make sure you do not add more than a 1cm (½in) layer at any one time because this will suffocate the grass. If the hollows are deeper than this you will have to make several topdressings, spaced out over the course of a growing season so that the grass has time to grow up through the topdressing between applications. Alternatively, spread out applications over several seasons to achieve a perfectly level surface to your lawn.

Humps need to be tackled individually. Using a sharp spade or half-moon edging iron, make an H-shaped cut into the lawn with the cross-bar of the H cutting through the hump you are trying to correct. Then, carefully undercut the turf from this cut and peel back the grass on either side to leave an oblong area of soil exposed. Take away soil as necessary to correct the hump before firming and replacing the peeled-back turves. Firm again with the back of your spade and check that the area is now even using a straight-edged piece of timber as a guide. Finally, fill any cracks with a 50:50 mixture of sieved garden soil and sharp sand, before watering well. This method can also be used to deal with hollows, adding sieved topsoil to raise the level rather than taking soil away.

Early autumn is the ideal time for essential lawn maintenance after a summer's hard wear and tear. Sharp edges against beds and borders will greatly improve the lawn's appearance.

Bare patches

Whether they are caused by heavy use or excessive shade from overhanging shrubs the solution to bare patches is basically the same. If they are caused by heavy wear you will need to relieve any compaction first by spiking. If shade is the problem you will need to cut back or thin out the overhanging foliage and use a shade-tolerant seed mixture when you resow. Following this preparation, prick over the bare patch with a garden fork and apply a well-balanced, all-purpose fertilizer, gently working it into the surface layer. Level and scatter grass seed at the rate of 20–35g per square metre

(1–1½oz per square yard), then cover the seed with a light scattering of sieved garden soil. Water well and cover with bird-proof netting. Keep well watered until the grass seedlings are well established.

Broken and uneven edges

Although broken or uneven edges can occur on any lawn, they are a particular problem in gardens with a light sandy soil, where the entire lawn edge may need to be recut every year. You can install a mowing strip along the edges (see page 28). Isolated broken edges are easy to repair by turning around a section of turf.

DEALING WITH UNEVEN EDGES

You can tidy an uneven edge at any time, but doing it in autumn will relieve the pressure at busier times of year. Hold a half-moon edger against a board held in position with your feet. This is not usually an annual job.

Planting container bulbs

Spring-flowering bulbs are an excellent choice for containers because they provide eye-catching colour early in the year and can be cleared out after flowering so that the pots and tubs can be used for summer bedding displays. You can also combine bulbs in permanent displays with trees, shrubs and perennials. Choose just one or two varieties in complementary or contrasting colours rather than a haphazard mixture.

Getting started

Almost any container will do provided it has drainage holes so that it doesn't get waterlogged, but for larger bulbs it will need to be at least 20cm (8in) deep. Most bulbs can be potted up using an all-purpose potting compost (soil mix), but for permanent displays use a loam-based compost, such as John Innes No. 2, which will keep its structure for longer. Plant bulbs at the normal recommended planting depth for permanent displays, but you can get away with shallower planting for temporary displays as long as each bulb is planted at least one bulb's depth below the surface. For large-flowered bulbs, make sure the container is stable with a wide base, so that it will not topple over in strong winds.

Take care that the compost does not dry out, and this may mean watering in winter. Add a mulch to conserve moisture and also to keep down weeds.

Bulbs and spring bedding

Some of the best container displays for spring combine bulbs with spring-flowering bedding plants, such as forget-me-nots (*Myosotis*), double daisies (*Bellis*) and polyanthus (*Primula*). This is often more effective than filling the container with bulbs alone, and it means that the container looks less bleak after planting, while the period of flowering is greatly extended. Put the plants in first, then the bulbs between them. If you plant the bulbs first, it can be difficult to remember their positions, and they are likely to be disturbed when you insert the plants.

Bulbs for impact

Displays of spring bulbs are less predictable than those of summer flowers, and it can be especially disappointing when different bulbs planted in the same container flower at different times. The consolation is that this does at least extend the period of interest. A good alternative is to plant single-subject displays

PLANTING BULBS FOR A SPRING WINDOW BOX

1 Cover the drainage holes with a layer of material to prevent the compost (soil mix) from falling out when you water and to aid drainage, such as broken pots or pieces of chipped bark (sold for mulching).

2 Add a 2.5cm (1in) layer of compost. Unless the planting is to be permanent, you can mix in some old compost previously used for summer bedding, since bulbs do not need a lot of nutrients.

3 You can pack in more bulbs by planting in layers. Place large bulbs, such as daffodils or tulips, at the lower level. Space them slightly apart so you can trickle compost in between the bulbs. Add more compost.

4 Position the smaller bulbs, such as crocuses and scillas, so that they lie between the larger bulbs. Small crocuses will be swamped by tall daffodils, so choose miniature or dwarf daffodils to keep a suitable balance.

5 Top up with more compost, but leave 2.5cm (1in) of space at the top for watering and perhaps a decorative mulch. Because the windowbox will look bare for some months, add winter-flowering pansies for interest.

PLANTING A PERMANENT CONTAINER

1 For a container with year-round interest, you can base the display on permanent evergreens such as dwarf conifers and ivies. The gaps can then be filled with colourful bulbs, followed by bedding plants, if you like.

2 Position the bulbs on the surface so that they are evenly spaced around the edge. Dwarf bulbs that multiply freely, such as scillas, chionodoxas, and *Anemone blanda*, will usually improve year after year.

3 Plant the bulbs with a trowel and water well. If adding bulbs to a container with established plants, try not to disturb the roots; the same applies if you add bedding plants later.

that, although often brief, are frequently bolder. By planting *en masse* and cramming in lots more bulbs you can enhance the overall display, especially if you are using small bulbs, such as crocus, grape hyacinths, scilla and chionodoxa, which can be planted almost touching. Larger bulbs, such as daffodils, hyacinths and tulips, are better spaced slightly, leaving at least half a bulb's width between bulbs.

Longer-lasting displays

Tubs, large pots and urns allow you to be more creative with your plant combinations. You can plant bulbs around permanent deciduous or evergreen shrubs or in multiple layers that flower at different times so that you get a continuity of flowers over a longer period. In a single container you could combine an early-spring-flowering crocus with a mid-spring-flowering dwarf daffodil and late-spring-flowering tulip to give a display through the entire season. Choose bulbs that should be planted at different depths. In this example, the tulips would be planted 15cm (6in) below the surface, the daffodils 10cm (4in), and the crocuses 5cm (2in).

PLANTING A LATE SPRING CONTAINER

1 Choose a large pot, and cover the drainage holes with broken crocks. Add a layer of grit for extra drainage. Tulips like a very well-drained compost (soil mix), so it is a good idea to mix some grit into the compost too. Part-fill the container, allowing room for the tulips to be planted under twice their own depth of compost.

2 Tulips are usually planted in late autumn or early winter, to reduce the risk of disease, but in a container the risks are minimal and they can safely be planted now. Choose a late-flowering variety, and arrange them on the compost, nose upwards. Cover with more compost, bringing the level to within 2.5cm (1in) of the rim of the pot.

3 Wallflowers should flower about the same time as late-flowering tulips. Choose a complementary colour, preferably scented. If bought in a bunch, separate them carefully before planting, and choose those with the best root systems if you have too many.

4 Plant the wallflowers above the tulips, firming the compost gently around the roots. Water the container well, and allow to drain. It should be kept just moist, but not too wet, throughout the winter, and watered more frequently when growth begins.

Naturalizing bulbs

Growing bulbs in a natural setting where they can be left undisturbed to spread and multiply is not only one of the most effective ways of growing them but is undoubtedly the easiest. The bulbs will flower year after year with the minimum of maintenance, adding interest to otherwise dull areas. You can naturalize bulbs in lawns, in borders and under the canopy of trees.

Naturalizing in grass

Choose bulbs that are adapted to the use you wish to put them to. Most bulb catalogues provide useful advice and there are often special deals on cultivars that have been bought in bulk for naturalizing.

You will need an area of grass that you don't mind leaving unmown until early summer to allow bulb foliage to die back naturally. In a small garden, the best bulbs to choose are those that flower in late winter or early spring, such as snowdrops and most crocuses. These should have died down almost completely by the time you are ready to give the lawn its first cut of the season. Alternatively, if you like to start mowing early, grow them towards the edge of the lawn where they can be appreciated and yet allowed to die down naturally after flowering. In these areas you'll be able to include bulbs such as daffodils, fritillaries and grape hyacinths.

Naturalizing in beds and borders

Areas that are regularly cultivated for planting seasonal bedding, for example, are not really suitable for naturalizing bulbs because you are likely to dig up the dormant bulbs by mistake unless they are clearly marked. But areas that are left

NATURALIZING BULBS INDIVIDUALLY IN GRASS

1 Scatter the bulbs on to the turf in a random fashion and plant them where they fall, but try to allow a distance of about 8–20cm (3–8in) between each one.

2 Dig a deep, square hole of about a spade's width and about 25cm (10in) deep, depending on the size of the bulb. You may need to go deeper than one spade's depth.

3 Put a layer of grit or sand in the bottom of the hole, then plant the bulb, base down. Cover the bulb with loose soil and replace the top divot. Firm down gently.

4 A special bulb-planting tool, which takes out a core of soil, will save time if you want to plant a lot of bulbs individually. Scatter the bulbs randomly as before.

5 Push the bulb planter into the soil, twisting it a little if the ground is hard, then pull it out with the core of soil. Release the core of soil and place the bulb at the bottom of the hole.

6 Pull off a little soil from the base of the core (to allow for the depth of the bulb), then replace the core in the hole. Firm gently. Fill any gaps with sieved garden soil.

relatively undisturbed, such as between shrubs and trees, can be effectively planted with naturalized bulbs. They will do particularly well between late-leafing deciduous specimens, where they can get plenty of light during early spring. Naturalized bulbs also combine well with late emerging perennials and hardy ferns, because these plants will help disguise the yellowing bulb foliage as they grow. Choose bulbs such as winter aconites, anemones, bluebells, grape hyacinths, crocuses, daffodils, fritillaries, snowdrops and chionodoxas.

Saving tender bulbs

Do not discard your dahlias – lift the tubers before frosts penetrate the ground and store them for next year. Even seed-raised plants will have formed tubers that you can store. Lift the dahlia tubers once the first frosts have blackened the foliage. Use a fork to lift the tubers, to minimize the risk of damaging them. Cut the old stem off to leave a stump about 5cm (2in) long. Stand the tubers upside-down so that moisture drains easily from the hollow stems. Using a mesh support is a convenient way to allow them to dry off. Keep in a dry, frost-free place. After a few days the tubers should be dry enough to store. Remove surplus soil, trim off loose bits of old roots and shorten the stem to leave a stump. Label each plant and dust with fungicide. Pack the tubers in a well-insulated box with peat, vermiculite, wood shavings, or crumpled newspaper placed between them.

A spare bedroom or cool but frost-free garage are suitable places for storage. Keep bulbs, corms and tubers where you can easily check them about once a month to make sure they are all still sound. If you notice any signs of rot, remove and destroy the affected tubers.

NATURALIZING BULBS IN SMALL AREAS OF GRASS

1 If you have a lot of small bulbs, such as crocuses and winter aconites (*Eranthis*), to plant in a limited area use a spade or half-moon edger to make an H-shaped cut.

2 Slice beneath the grass with a spade until you can fold back the turf for planting. Do this with care to get an even turf that can be folded back without cracking.

3 Loosen the ground before planting, as it may be very compacted. If you want to apply a slow-acting fertilizer, such as bonemeal, work it into the soil at the same time.

4 Avoid planting in rows or regimented patterns. You want the bulbs to look natural and informal, so scatter them and plant more or less where they fall.

5 For larger bulbs, make deeper holes with a trowel. Plant them so that they are covered with about twice their own depth of soil. Use a spade to dig out a hole for a group of bulbs.

6 Firm the soil, then return the grass. Firm again if necessary to make sure it is flat, and water if the weather is dry to make sure that the grass grows again quickly.

Planting new shrubs and hedges

Autumn is the best time to plant most shrubs and hedges, since they will need less watering than those planted in spring. The main exception are evergreens, which should be planted in mid- to late spring so that they are not exposed to cold, drying winds before they become established. Now is also a good time to prune rambling roses, which can quickly become very large if not kept under control.

Adding new plants

In autumn the existing garden displays are still fresh in your mind, so you will be in a better position to decide what new additions you need.

Do not prune rambling roses in the first year, but thereafter prune in autumn after flowering by removing any dead or diseased shoots and reducing sideshoots by about two-thirds.

PRUNING A RAMBLING ROSE

1 Prune a rambling rose after flowering but while the new shoots are still fairly pliable. Older, congested plants can be more off-putting than younger ones, but all ramblers are fairly straightforward to prune.

2 First, cut out any dead or damaged shoots or those that are very weak and spindly. Do not remove very vigorous, young shoots. Work methodically, cutting shoots back in sections.

3 Cut out old stems that have flowered, but only where there are new shoots to replace them. Shorten the sideshoots on old stems that have been retained (those that have flowered) by about two-thirds.

4 Tie in the flexible shoots to the support. Wherever possible, tie loosely to horizontal wires or a trellis. This will prevent the whippy shoots from being caught by the wind and getting damaged or harming others.

And because it is not a busy time of year in most gardens, it means you have plenty of time to consider all the options and are less likely to make mistakes.

One of the most common pitfalls when adding new shrubs to a bed or border is to plant them too close together. This means that you will either have to move one or more shrubs when they get overcrowded in a few years, or spend a lot of time pruning them to keep them within bounds. But don't be tempted to buy large specimens to fill the borders and create an instant effect. Not only is this expensive, but older plants will not establish as quickly and will soon be overtaken by the faster-growing smaller plants.

If you are planting a completely new bed of shrubs, fill the gaps between with fast-growing plants, such as buddleia and mock orange, which will quickly grow and provide a colourful display while the slower-growing permanent shrubs are getting established and filling out. The filler plants can then be removed as necessary over the following

PLANTING A HEDGE

1 Prepare the ground thoroughly, as a hedge will be there for a long time and this is your only opportunity to improve the soil. Clear it of all weeds and their roots and dig deeply.

2 Take out a trench about 25cm (10in) deep. Set up a line of garden twine to make sure that the row is straight. Place the excavated soil to one side of the trench.

3 Add as much well-rotted garden compost or manure as you can spare, then fork it into the base of the trench to improve the soil and encourage deep rooting.

4 Return the soil to the trench, adding more organic material as you do so. Then apply bonemeal and rake it in. Don't apply fast-acting fertilizers at this time of year.

5 Bare-root hedging comes bundled together, with the roots in a bag of peat or soil. If you cannot plant immediately, simply dig the hedging into a spare piece of ground.

6 Dig large holes at the appropriate spacing. A typical spacing is 38–45cm (15–18in), but it may be different for some plants, so always check the recommended spacing first.

7 Check that the plants are set at the correct depth and firm them in well, treading around them to remove any large air pockets, which could cause the roots to dry out.

8 Water thoroughly, and be prepared to water regularly in dry spells for the first year. Protect new hedging with a windbreak in exposed gardens.

seasons. The second option is to smother the ground between the shrubs with complementary groundcover plants underplanted with colourful bulbs. Or you could plug the gaps with a sowing of hardy annuals in spring. These will grow and flower in their first year before dying in autumn. Most will readily self-seed so you won't need to sow afresh each spring. They will also die out naturally as the permanent shrubs take over the bed, using up the available light, moisture and nutrients.

Container-grown or bare-root?
Most garden plants are sold in containers, which are convenient because they needn't be planted immediately. Some trees and shrubs (particularly hedges and roses) ordered by mail order from specialist nurseries may arrive bare-root, however, with their roots wrapped in moss and a protective sleeve. These are plants that have been lifted from the field; they are often cheaper than container-grown and can be just as good if planted promptly. Bare-root plants are also sometimes available at garden centres and other outlets.

Autumn pond care

Although ponds need little routine maintenance, there are a few end-of-season tasks that are essential if you want to keep your plants and fish (if any) in good condition. Clear out any dead or dying plant material, which will rot and foul the water over the winter. Overgrown plants can be trimmed back, but leave removed material on the side of the pond overnight so that any trapped pond creatures have a chance to make their way back to the water.

Fallen leaves

Stop autumn leaves getting into the pond by covering it with a fine-mesh net held taut above the water. If leaves congregate on the netting, clear them away to prevent the net from sagging into the water. Large ponds that are too big to net can be protected by erecting a low, fine-mesh fence around the perimeter to catch any wind-blown leaves. Clear these up regularly and turn them into leafmould.

Tender aquatics

Some aquatic plants, such as the water lettuce (*Pistia stratiotes*) and *Salvinia auriculata*, will be killed by frost, even though they can multiply rapidly outdoors in summer. Fairy moss (*Azolla filiculoides*) sometimes survives a mild winter in favourable areas, but as an insurance policy overwinter a few plants in a frost-free place. Net a few plants that are still in good condition. They may already be deteriorating in the cooler weather, so don't save any that appear to be rotting or badly damaged. Put a handful of the plants into a plastic container – such as lunch box or ice cream container – full of water. Don't cram them in so that they are overcrowded. Use extra containers rather than have all the plants touching. Some gardeners put a little soil in the bottom to provide nutrients. Keep the plants in a warm, light place, such as a heated greenhouse. You might also be able to keep them on a well-lit windowsill. Top up or change the water occasionally to prevent it from becoming stagnant.

Miniature waterlilies

With the exception of tropical waterlilies, which are usually only

An established, well-balanced pond needs little additional work in autumn, but carrying out a few seasonal tasks now will keep it in good order and help prepare it for the winter months ahead.

AVOIDING ROTTING LEAVES IN THE POND

1 Protect the pond from the worst of the leaf fall with a fine-mesh net. Anchor it just above the surface of the pond. Remove the leaves regularly, and eventually remove the netting.

2 If you are not able to cover your pond with a net or don't like the appearance of one, use a fish net or rake to remove leaves regularly to prevent them rotting and fouling the water.

3 Trim back dead or dying plants from around the edge of the pond, especially where the vegetation is likely to fall into the water, where it will decompose.

grown by enthusiasts with heated pools, waterlilies are very hardy and are usually planted deep enough not to come to any harm in cold weather. Miniature waterlilies are sometimes used for raised miniature pools, in a half-barrel or shrub tub for example, and these are vulnerable. Because the container is raised above the ground, in very severe weather the water can freeze solid throughout. Try wrapping your pool in several layers of bubble insulation material, or move it into a cool greenhouse for the winter.

Protect pond pumps

If you leave a pump in your pond over winter, ice may damage it. Remove submersible pumps from the water before penetrating frosts cause the water to freeze deeply. Don't just take the pump out of the pond and leave it where moisture can enter – it should be stored in a dry place. Clean the pump before you put it away. It will probably be covered with algae which can be scrubbed off. Remove the filter and either replace it or clean it. Follow the

manufacturer's instructions. Make sure all the water is drained from the pump. If your pump is an external one, check that the system is drained. Read the manufacturer's instructions, and carry out any other servicing necessary before storing the pump in a dry place over winter. It may be necessary to send it away for a service, in which case do it now instead of waiting until spring. Replace the pond pump with a pond heater during the winter to prevent the surface of the pond freezing over.

OVERWINTERING TENDER AQUATICS

1 Net a few plants in good condition. They may already be deteriorating in the cooler weather, so don't save any that appear to be rotting or badly damaged.

2 Put a handful of the plants in a plastic container of pond water. Don't overcrowd them – use extra containers rather than allow them to touch. Some gardeners put a little soil in the bottom to provide nutrients.

3 Keep the plants in a light, frost-free place, such as a greenhouse. You might be able to keep them on a cool windowsill. Top up or change the water occasionally so that it does not become stagnant.

Creating winter interest

Filling containers with winter-flowering plants is one of the quickest and easiest ways of brightening up your garden. Whether positioned on the patio or placed next to a well-used path or doorway, they'll give months of pleasure when little else in the garden is providing interest. It's also worth having a few winter containers where you can see them from the house. For example, you could plant up a winter hanging basket and even a window box outside the kitchen window to add a little sparkle to the view.

Recycling plants

You don't need to spend lots of money on new plants each autumn because many garden plants can be given a temporary home in a garden container for the winter months. Self-seeded hellebores and rooted runners and sideshoots from groundcover plants, such as ajugas and bergenias, as well as unwanted divisions from overgrown evergreen perennials that have been divided earlier in the year, can all be used.

Some plants can be saved and recycled from summer displays, too. For example, the small-leaved ivies used in hanging baskets and as trailers around the edge of summer containers can be reused in almost any winter arrangement. Similarly, the hardy grey-leaved senecio (*Senecio cineraria*), which is often included in bedding displays, can be used to add interest to winter containers, too.

Winter containers are of particular value because there is little else to catch the eye. Here, pansies and variegated ivy have been combined for a long-lasting display.

Adding seasonal fillers

Many evergreen shrubs and perennials are worth buying for winter containers. These days garden centres sell them as very small plants so they will not take up too much space. Shrubs with colourful foliage, such as cultivars of *Euonymus fortunei*, or small-leaved hebes will provide colour and structure to the arrangement. A few berrying plants are worth adding, such as the superb *Skimmia japonica* subsp. *reevesiana* with its compact clusters of bright red fruit that last all winter, or pink-berried pernettyas, which look a treat when accompanied by pink and white winter-flowering dwarf heathers. In a larger container you could try winter-flowering jasmine, small upright and prostrate conifers, or *Viburnum tinus*, which flowers for a long period from late winter.

Whatever the weather, make sure you water the container or basket from time to time, throughout the winter months, so that the plants do not run short of moisture.

PLANTING A WINTER HANGING BASKET

1 Line the hanging basket with a suitable organic material. Conifer branches, as shown here, are an ideal material.

2 Fill the lined basket with a suitable potting compost (soil mix) to about one-third of its depth, spreading it evenly over the base.

3 Position the plants first to see how they will look. Fill in the spaces between the plants with more potting compost.

4 Any gaps between the plants can be filled with small bulbs or bedding plants to provide a riot of spring colour.

PLANTING A WINTER WINDOW BOX

1 Assemble all the necessary materials. These include the window box, crocks, a good potting compost (soil mix) and the plants. If the box is light, assemble it on the ground. If not, then assemble it in position.

2 Holes in the bottom are essential to allow good drainage. Stop the compost from being washed out by placing crocks over these. If very good drainage is needed, then a layer of gravel can also be added.

3 Partially fill the box with compost, gently tapping the sides to make sure that no air gaps remain. Never over-firm soil-less potting mixes, which can become waterlogged and airless, and the plants will suffer.

4 Place the plants on the compost to work out the arrangement and check their positions before finally planting. Make sure that they are planted in the compost at the same depth that they were in their pots or trays. Plant them fairly close for an instant effect.

5 A selection of small bulbs will make a useful additional display for the window box. The bulbs can be planted in among the main plants and are best planted in groups of three so that they give a fuller display. Water the basket thoroughly once it is planted.

6 Top up the window box with compost so that the surface is about 2.5cm (1in) below the rim to allow for easy watering. Add a layer of gravel to prevent soil from splashing against the leaves. Water well and keep watering as necessary throughout the winter months.

Giving a colour boost

Winter-flowering bedding plants and the earliest of the spring bulbs can be combined to create an ever-changing and colourful display right through the winter months. Winter bedding plants are sometimes disappointing as some varieties tend to flower only in mild spells. For the best performance in cold weather, choose the many colours of the Universal Series of winter-flowering pansy and Crescendo Series polyanthus. They can be bought in mixed or single colours so you can create complementary or colour-coordinated schemes. Choose stocky plants that are just coming into flower so that you can be sure of the colour.

Ornamental cabbages are another good source of winter colour, with rosettes of leaves variegated in pink, cream, white and green.

Late winter-flowering bulbs are well worth adding at planting time to extend the display into spring. Crocus, scilla, snowdrops, dwarf daffodils and tulips are worth including. You can also drop in some ready flowering potted bulbs which are available from garden centres in early spring, to give winter containers a fillip.

Keep winter-flowering pansies in a sheltered position if you want continuous colour through the winter months.

Overwintering tender plants

Many tender perennials, such as marguerites and osteospermums, which are widely used in summer containers and bedding schemes, can be successfully overwintered and used as the basis for displays next year. This could save you a great deal of money and will give you the chance to keep unusual plants from year to year. There are several ways you can overwinter tender perennials, but the method you choose will depend on the species you are trying to overwinter.

In the border

Some plants, including *Senecio cineraria*, chocolate cosmos, daturas, fuchsias and penstemons, are almost hardy and can be given sufficient protection outside in the garden in most areas. Once the foliage has died back, cover the ground with a deep mulch of dry leaves or chipped bark to provide insulation. In an exposed garden net the pile or surround it with pieces of wood to keep it in place. On lighter soils, you can even bury plants such as fuchsias and pelargoniums in shallow trenches to provide the insulation cover. Dig a trench about 30cm (12in) deep, line it with straw, then lay the plants on this. Cover the plants with more straw and return the soil. Dig them up in spring, pot them up and keep in warmth and good light to start into growth again. If the winters are not too harsh, many of the plants should survive.

In a coldframe

The protection offered by a coldframe will allow you to overwinter a larger range of plants, including *Calceolaria integrifolia*, diascias, glechomas, helichrysums and verbenas. Insulate the sides and top of the coldframe with layers of bubble plastic or blocks of polystyrene (styrofoam). The plants can be planted or packed in boxes. Check them periodically and remove any dying foliage. Water if necessary during mild spells in late winter and early spring.

In the shed

Frost-free sheds and garages are suitable for overwintering all the above plants, as well as tuberous begonias, cannas and impatiens.

OVERWINTERING PELARGONIUMS

1 Lift the plants before the first frost if possible, though they will often survive a light frost if you take them in promptly afterwards.

2 Shake as much of the soil off the roots as possible, to minimize the amount of space the plants will take up in storage.

3 Trim the longest roots back to about 5–8cm (2–3in) long, to make potting up easier. Also remove any damaged foliage.

4 Shorten the shoots to about 10cm (4in), and trim off any remaining leaves. Although this looks drastic, new shoots will grow in spring, and you will be able to use these for cuttings if you want more plants.

5 The most effective way to store pelargoniums for the winter is in large trays at least 15cm (6in) deep. Half-fill with potting compost (soil mix), position the plants and add more compost to cover the roots.

6 If you want to overwinter your pelargoniums on a windowsill indoors, you may find it more convenient to use large pots instead of trays. Water well initially, then only when the compost becomes almost dry.

OVERWINTERING TENDER FUCHSIAS

1 If your fuchsias have been grown in pots during the summer, take them into the greenhouse. If planted in the ground, lift with a fork and remove excess soil.

2 Pot up the plants individually, or in large boxes if you have a lot of plants, then put them in a frost-free place, such as in the greenhouse or on a light windowsill indoors.

3 Tidy up the plants by removing old leaves and pinching out any soft green tips. You must keep the plants cool but frost-free. Water sparingly when the soil is almost dry.

Trim the plants back and pack them in wooden boxes or trays filled with a mixture of equal parts potting compost (soil mix) and sharp sand. To prevent the roots drying out, line the box with perforated plastic sheeting beforehand. Check occasionally to make sure the compost doesn't dry out completely.

In the greenhouse

All tender perennials can be overwintered if you have a greenhouse. If it is unheated, you can overwinter all the plants listed so far plus euryops, felicias, gazanias and lobelias. Place the plants in an insulated box after trimming them back.

In the house

Indoors you can overwinter the most valuable and unusual tender perennials. Pot them up into containers that are large enough to accommodate their rootballs. Keep them somewhere light but out of direct sun in a cool room that is free of frost – an unheated bedroom, porch or conservatory is ideal. This is the best way of overwintering precious plants and other prized specimens.

Cuttings

Fuchsias and pelargoniums can be rooted from cuttings taken in spring or autumn. If you are overwintering old plants, you can use them to provide plenty of cuttings in spring. If you took cuttings in late summer or the autumn, however, your young plants will still be growing actively. Make sure that you keep these plants in good light and reasonably warm – they will then probably retain their foliage. If conditions are favourable, pelargoniums may even flower during the winter months.

Tender fuchsias that are being grown outside can be overwintered in a frost-free place indoors and will provide early cutting material for new plants in spring.

Tidying up in autumn

By late autumn there will be plenty of weeding and tidying up to keep you busy in the garden. You should continue to clear the fallen leaves from the lawn and also the beds and borders. If you allow fallen leaves to lie for long on small plants, such as alpines, the plants may begin to rot due to the lack of light and free movement of air. If leaves are left on the ground, they can damage areas of grass and the blanket of leaves will also provide a haven for slugs and other pests that will eat your plants. Don't wait until most of the leaves have fallen from the trees, before you go round and pick them away from vulnerable plants; you should remove the leaves as soon as you notice them.

Autumn-flowering border chrysanthemums will need to be lifted and protected in winter unless your garden is in a particularly mild and sheltered area.

LIFTING AND PROTECTING CHRYSANTHEMUMS

1 Lift the roots after the plants have finished flowering and before severe frosts arrive.

2 Shake surplus soil off the roots before bringing them indoors.

3 Trim the tops off and cut any long, straggly roots back to keep the rootball compact. Place a layer of just damp soil or compost (soil mix) in a box or tray about 10cm (4in) deep. Dust the roots with fungicide.

4 Position the roots on top of the compost and cover them with about 2.5cm (1in) of soil, firming lightly. Don't forget to label the plants. Keep the box in a cool, light place. Keep the soil slightly damp but not wet.

Essential tasks

Weeding is particularly important now because any weeds that are left will set seed and cause even more problems next year. After weeding, apply a generous mulch, about 8cm (3in) deep, of well-rotted organic matter over the soil to help insulate the ground from the winter cold. If you cannot apply mulch over all your borders, concentrate it around plants that are of borderline hardiness to help them survive the winter outdoors. It's also your last chance to protect tender plants by bringing in containers and lifting stools and tubers. Lift tender perennials growing in the garden and pot them up or overwinter them in boxes somewhere frost-free. If you like a tidy garden over the winter, cut back the dying foliage on most herbaceous perennials now. However, leave those that have produced attractive seedheads to provide much needed winter interest and a place for overwintering beneficial insects such as ladybirds (ladybugs) to hide.

POTTING UP WINTER ACONITES

1 Winter aconites (*Eranthis hyemalis*) can be quite hard to find in border soil because at first they just look like lumps of earth. By late autumn, however, the buds will be showing, and where tubers have matured they can grow to as much as 3–4cm (1¼–1½) across.

2 Prepare a small pot with drainage material, such as pieces of polystyrene (styrofoam) or broken crocks, and a soil-based compost (soil mix) and replant one large tuber 5cm (2in) below the surface. Cover with more compost and water well, mulching the top if wished.

3 Place the pot outdoors on your windowsill or in a group with other winter-flowering specimens on a patio table where they will give welcome colour to the winter garden. After blooming, they can be replanted beneath a deciduous shrub or tree.

Leaving the growth on herbaceous perennials until early spring also provides winter protection for the underground crown, which is an important consideration in colder areas.

Don't be in too much of a hurry to throw away plants from your summer bedding displays. Some of the most popular plants are perennial and can be kept to provide a bigger and better display next year, and ageratums, argyranthemums, bidens, busy Lizzies, diascias and petunias are all worth potting up. Trim the plants back so they do not take up too much space and to make them easier to handle, pot them up and keep them in a frost-free place. In mid-spring they will start to shoot, when they can be potted up to produce large specimens, or you can propagate new plants from cuttings of the fresh new shoots.

stored, and even those outdoor ones that flower later are best treated this way. Even those that tolerate some frost are more likely to survive if kept fairly dry. Wet and cold is the combination to avoid.

Dispose of your rubbish...wisely

Gardeners always acquire a lot of rubbish and debris in the autumn, and there is no simple way to deal with it all. Be environmentally friendly and recycle as much as possible through composting. Some things are best disposed of elsewhere or burned – diseased material and pernicious perennial weeds for instance, as well as woody material if you don't have a shredder. An incinerator that will burn the rubbish quickly is preferable to a traditional smoky bonfire. A large quantity of leaves is better turned into leafmould. Some leaves rot down slowly, but the end product is particularly useful for adding to potting mixtures.

Overwintering chrysanthemums

There are many kinds of chrysanthemum, but it is only the autumn-flowering chrysanthemums that are likely to cause confusion when it comes to overwintering. In mild, frost-free climates they can all be left in the ground, and many of the species, such as *Chrysanthemum zawadskii*, are hardy even in cold areas. But in temperate climates the highly bred, early-flowering autumn chrysanthemums are best lifted and

Winter aconites (*Eranthis hyemalis*) can be potted up now to provide a wonderful fillip to winter garden displays.

Planting trees

It is essential to plant a new tree well if it is to establish quickly. Making sure the roots are secure in the soil and never run short of moisture are the two key components to successful planting. Most trees are sold in containers these days and can be planted at any time of the year but will establish more quickly if planted in autumn when the soil is moist and still warm. Bare-root trees are best planted in autumn.

Spacing

Like shrubs, trees need to be spaced at the correct distance if they are not to cause trouble later on. You will need to find out the approximate mature height of adjacent trees (by looking on the plant labels or consulting a good plant encyclopedia) and using the following simple calculation: add the heights together and then divide by two for the correct planting distance. For example, if you are planting a tree that will reach 15m (45ft) alongside a tree that will reach 11m (33ft), they should be planted 13m (39ft) apart (11m + 15m = 26m, 26m ÷ 2 = 13m; 45ft + 33ft = 78ft, 78ft ÷ 2 = 39ft).

Trees should always be planted well away from your house and other buildings, otherwise their roots may interfere with underground drains and the foundations and, in extreme cases, cause subsidence. As a rule, don't plant most trees nearer than their mature height. Some types of trees, such as poplars and willows, have more questing roots than others, so plant these even further away.

Planting

After preparing the ground by digging thoroughly and removing perennial weeds and other debris, excavate a planting hole about twice as wide and a little deeper than the rootball of the tree you are planting. On heavy soils, prick the sides of the hole to break up any clay so that the roots are not prevented from growing out into the surrounding soil. Then add well-rotted organic matter or proprietary planting mixture and lightly fork it into the soil at the bottom of the hole. After watering the rootball thoroughly, position it in the hole and check the depth using a cane – the tree should be at the same depth as it was in the pot or ground (look for a change in bark colour on bare-rooted trees). Trim damaged roots from bare-root trees and uncoil any circling roots at the base of container-grown specimens. Reposition the rootball in the hole, then add about 15cm (6in) of excavated soil while keeping the trunk upright. Shake bare-rooted trees to make sure that soil trickles

National tree planting week occurs in late autumn each year, and this is an ideal time to plant deciduous specimens, while the soil is still warm and moist.

PLANTING A TREE

1 Place a strong stake of rot-resistant wood or one treated with preservative in the hole, knocking it in so that it cannot move.

2 Place the tree in the hole, pushing the rootball up against the stake, so that the stem and stake are 8–10cm (3–4in) apart.

3 Backfill with soil and firm it down around the tree with the heel of your shoe. Top up with soil if necessary.

4 Although it is possible to use string, proper adjustable rose or tree ties with a spacer provide the best type of support. Fix the lower one 15cm (6in) above the soil level.

5 Fix the second tie near the top of the stake, slightly below the head of the tree. Do not make the tie so tight around the stem that it will constrict expansion as sap flows in spring.

6 Water the ground around the tree thoroughly and mulch the surface of the soil with chipped bark, well-rotted organic matter or a proprietory plant mulching mat.

between the roots, thus avoiding air pockets. Firm, and then add the next layer of soil. Repeat the process until the hole is filled. Water thoroughly and mulch with a thick layer of well-rotted organic matter.

Staking

If the tree is over 1.5m (5ft) tall it should be staked to prevent it being blown about in the wind. Drive a sturdy 1.5m (5ft) stake into the hole before planting, to leave about 60cm (24in) above the surface after planting. Position the stake slightly off-centre and on the windward side of the tree. After planting, attach the stake to the tree using adjustable tree ties, one at the top and one close to the ground. Container-grown trees may be better staked after planting by driving the stake in at an angle to avoid damaging the rootball.

Recommended trees

Acer griseum
Amelanchier lamarckii
Betula pendula 'Youngii'
Crataegus laevigata 'Paul's Scarlet'
Fagus sylvatica 'Purpurea Pendula'
Malus 'John Downie'
Prunus cerasifera 'Nigra'
Pyrus salicifolia 'Pendula'
Rhus typhina
Sorbus 'Joseph Rock'

Propagating plants

Late autumn is an ideal time for taking cuttings of many plants, particularly if you are short of time. Hardwood cuttings root more slowly than most softwood or semi-ripe cuttings, which you can take in spring and summer, but they need less attention. Most don't need heat, and because you plant them in the open ground (or in a coldframe), watering won't be onerous. Many plants experience a surge of root growth at this time of year, so cuttings taken now have a good chance of success.

Take hardwood cuttings

This is the best time to take hardwood cuttings of many popular trees and shrubs. Some will root in a prepared patch of ground, but most will root more quickly if covered by a coldframe. You could also try rooting a few of the more difficult subjects in a heated propagator.

Traditionally, hardwood cuttings 15–23cm (6–9in) long are taken in late autumn or early winter, depending on the type of growth the plant makes. Trim each cutting with a straight cut just below a leaf joint at

Deciduous ceanothus can be propagated from basal cuttings put in a coldframe.

the bottom and remove any soft growth towards the tip by cutting at an angle just above a bud. Prepare a slit or V-shaped trench and half-fill it with sharp sand or grit. Insert the cuttings 15cm (6in) apart so that the bottom two-thirds of each is buried. Firm the soil back around the cuttings and water well. In cold areas you can cover the cuttings with an open-ended cloche or coldframe. Keep well watered. Plant out rooted cuttings the following autumn.

Using a propagator

In a heated propagator, make the cuttings 10–15cm (4–6in) long and prepare in the same way. Evergreen shrubs, which are difficult to root outside, should have all but the top pair of leaves removed. Wounding the base of the cutting by scratching a little bark, about 1cm (½in), away from the base to one side, and dipping the base in hormone rooting powder can help to encourage rooting. Insert in pots full of cuttings compost (soil mix) and water well. Set the temperature for 15°C (59°F), reducing to 10°C (50°F) after a couple of weeks. Rooting should be complete by the time the propagator is needed in early spring.

Shrubs from cuttings

Hardwood cuttings are usually successful with *Buddleja* (butterfly bush), *Cornus alba* (dogwood), *Cornus stolonifera* (dogwood), *Deutzia*, *Forsythia*, *Ligustrum ovalifolium* (privet), *Philadelphus* (mock orange), *Ribes sanguineum* (flowering currant), roses (species and hybrids), *Salix* (willow), *Spiraea*, *Tamarix* (tamarisk), *Viburnum* (deciduous) and *Weigela*, among many others. *Aucuba japonica*, *Ceanothus* (deciduous) and *Hypericum* can be propagated from heel or basal

Buddleias are easy to root from hardwood cuttings taken during late autumn.

cuttings now. You should be prepared to experiment or consult a specialist book.

Trees from hardwood cuttings

Some trees can also be propagated from hardwood cuttings, and *Platanus* (plane), *Populus* (poplar) and *Salix* (willow) are particularly easy. If propagating trees, decide whether you want a multi-stemmed tree or one with a single main stem. If the latter, set the cuttings deeper in the trench so that the top bud is just below the surface of the soil.

Plant out layers and rooted cuttings

Rooted layers prepared in spring and hardwood cuttings inserted last year will be ready for planting out in their final positions if they have rooted well. They can be severed from their parent and then transplanted with as much soil around the roots as possible. Rooted cuttings can either be potted up to grow on or planted out in the garden. Poorly rooted layers can be left for another year.

TAKING HARDWOOD CUTTINGS

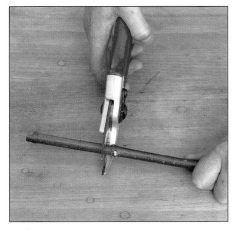

1 Choose stems that are firm and pencil thickness. The length of the cutting will depend on the plant, but about 15cm (6in) is appropriate for most. Make a cut straight across the stem, just below a node.

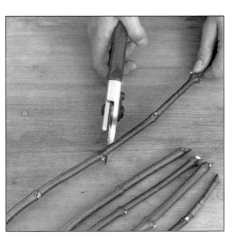

2 Using a pair of secateurs (pruners), make the second cut about 15cm (6in) above the first. Make the cut above a node, but this time at an angle so that you will know which is the top and which the bottom of the cutting.

3 Although a rooting hormone is not essential, it can increase the success rate, especially with plants that are difficult to root. Moisten the bases of the cuttings in water before dipping in the powder.

4 Dip the moistened base end of each cutting in the powder, then tap on a hard surface to remove any excess. Alternatively, you can use a liquid or get rooting hormone, in which case no water is needed.

5 Make a slit trench with a spade, a little shallower than the length of the cuttings. Choose an unobtrusive and fairly sheltered spot in the garden to leave the cuttings undisturbed for a year.

6 Sprinkle some grit or coarse sand in the base of the slit if the ground is poorly drained. This will help to prevent waterlogging around the cuttings. Firm lightly to make sure there are no air pockets.

7 Insert the cuttings 8–10cm (3–4in) apart, upright against the back of the slit, leaving about 2.5–5cm (1–2in) above the ground.

8 Firm the soil around the cuttings, to eliminate the pockets of air that would cause the cutting to dry out.

9 Water the cuttings and label. Continue to water them in dry weather, especially during the spring and summer months.

Providing winter protection

Extreme cold and wet are the two main killers in the winter garden. You can take steps now to protect your plants by putting up barriers, insulating roots, wrapping top-growth and keeping off the rain.

Protect against wind

Cold winds in winter and early spring are often the forgotten threat to borderline-hardy plants. They are particularly damaging to conifers that transpire throughout the winter months and can be scorched if there is insufficient water available to the roots – if the ground is frozen, for example. The risk is even greater if the plant has been planted recently

A blanket of snow will actually help prevent winter damage from cold by insulating underlying plants from the wind.

PROTECTING VULNERABLE SHRUBS

1 A little protection from cold winds and snow is all that many cold-sensitive shrubs require in areas where they are of borderline hardiness. Push cut branches of evergreens into the soil around the plant.

2 If the shrub is tall, you may also need to tie cut branches of evergreens, or fronds of bracken, so that they remain in position. Use fine-mesh netting or soft string for the purpose.

3 If you don't have a supply of evergreen shoots or bracken, use garden fleece or a woven mesh for protection. For extra protection, fold these over to give more than one thickness before tying into position.

4 Some shrubs are damaged by cold winds as much as low temperatures, and for these a windbreak will prevent wind scorch. Insert canes or stakes around the plant, then fix several layers of windbreak netting to these.

because the new specimen will not have had time to establish a good root system into the surrounding soil. The best way to protect individual plants from wind damage is to erect a windbreak. You can use a special fabric screen, held taut between strong posts that have been hammered into the ground. Make sure the windbreak is tall enough to protect the top of the plant and position it at least 15cm (6in) away from the plant to allow good air circulation. If you are protecting a hedge, put the windbreak on the windward side.

Protect against cold

Borderline-hardy plants, such as many climbers and wall shrubs, will need protecting during the coldest weather. Some will just need their vulnerable topgrowth wrapped in an insulating blanket of straw held in place with fine-mesh netting. But others will need their roots protecting too. Many shrubs and evergreen climbers that are being grown in a colder climate than their place of origin can be treated like herbaceous plants. This means their topgrowth is killed off by frost at the end of each growing season but their roots, which remain alive underground, produce new shoots the following spring. Widely grown examples include hardy fuchsias, passion flower and *Solanum crispum*.

The best way to protect the roots is to cover them with a 15cm (6in) deep mulch of bark chippings, compost or collected leaves. Keep the insulation layer in position by covering it with netting and pegging it down at the edges. Hedge trimmings can also be used in this way. Containers are also worth protecting from periods of freezing temperatures. Wrap the pot in a double layer of bubble plastic, and borderline hardy plants in a double layer of garden fleece. Make sure you stand the container on pot feet to prevent it becoming waterlogged and leave an access point to allow for easy watering during dry spells.

Wrap a windbreak around conifers growing in exposed positions to prevent wind scorch during the winter months.

PROTECTING NEWLY PLANTED EVERGREENS

1 Insert three strong canes or stakes at equal distances around the plant, then wrap a plastic sheet or several layers of garden fleece around the outside. Peg down the bottom and staple the sides together.

2 If you don't want to erect a long-term shield, perhaps on aesthetic grounds, cover the plant with a large plastic bag, pegged to the ground, but remove it when the worst of the weather is over.

PROTECTING DELICATE ALPINES

1 Some alpines with hairy leaves are likely to rot if they become too wet and waterlogged during the cold months. You can protect vulnerable alpines and other low-growing plants from winter wet by covering with a sheet of glass or rigid plastic substitute supported on special wires.

2 You can also use bricks and pebbles to support and weight the pane. If you have a spare cloche, perhaps not needed until spring, you might be able to use this to protect alpines. Leave the ends open, but make sure that the cloche is firmly anchored and not likely to be lifted by strong winds.

Protect against wet

Winter wet can cause plant casualties in any garden, and on heavy soils it is a killer. Some plants are particularly vulnerable, such as silver-leaved shrubs, perennials and low-growing alpines with hairy leaves. Even perfectly hardy plants, such as the Christmas rose (*Helleborus niger*), will benefit from the protection when in flower because heavy rain can spoil the winter blooms. Protect individual plants with open-ended cloches or, if small enough, a sheet of glass propped up on bricks. Use sheets of plastic to protect wall-trained peach trees from rain splash, which carries the disease peach leaf curl. Keep the sides open to allow pollinating insects in when in bloom during early spring and maintain good air circulation.

Cleaning up the greenhouse

Annual cleaning is essential to maintain the efficiency of the greenhouse: even a little dirt on the glass can make a significant difference to the amount of light that reaches the plants, and pests and diseases that are allowed to overwinter are more likely to become unmanageable the following year. If you can, it's always best to take advantage of the less busy season for the chore of cleaning, rather than waiting until you need to start sowing in spring. And any permanent plants in the greenhouse will benefit from the extra light during the dark days of winter.

Getting started

Choose a mild spell so that all the permanent plants can be stood outside without risk for a couple of days. Clear out any of the remaining crops and any debris as well as all temporary staging and shelving to leave the greenhouse as clear as possible. Take down all temporary shading material, and clear out any piles of empty pots, seed trays and unused bags of compost (soil mix). Deconstruct and disinfect watering systems, such as capillary matting, that are still in use. Turn off the electricity supply at the mains, and remove all electrical equipment.

Greenhouse structure

Using a suitable diluted disinfectant and a hard-bristle brush, scrub down all the internal surfaces in the greenhouse, including the floor, permanent benches and staging. Make sure you clean right into the corners, scrubbing the greenhouse base right up to the frame. Use a toothbrush to clean the mouldings of aluminium glazing bars and clean other areas with wire wool. Wash down the inside of the glass with

During a mild spell in autumn, take the plants that live year round in the greenhouse to a sheltered spot in the garden so that you can clean the greenhouse thoroughly.

disinfectant solution. Make sure the overlaps between panes of glass are cleared of algae, which reduce light transmission during the winter months. Use a plastic plant label or similar to scrape out stubborn moss and algae. Finally, rinse down the whole of the inside of the greenhouse with clean water from a hosepipe.

Clean any remaining shading wash from the outside of the greenhouse glass and use a floor mop or broom to wash down the outside of the roof with a household detergent. There is no need to sterilize the outside of the greenhouse. Wash the sides and ends and carry out any essential maintenance, such as replacing cracked panes of glass and clearing out the gutters.

Pots and seed trays

Clean all empty pots and seed trays that have been used during the course of the season using the same

diluted disinfectant (check that the product you are using is suitable for use on plastic, however). Scrub the insides to remove any remaining compost and rinse in clean water. Don't keep open bags of unused compost for next year's sowings because it will no longer be sterile. It is far better to buy fresh next year and use any waste compost as a soil improver when planting in the garden.

Greenhouse plants

Permanent plants that couldn't be removed from the greenhouse will need to be protected from the cleaning process under a sheet of plastic. Once the greenhouse is clean, remove the covering and inspect the plants to check for pests and diseases – removing any infected material. Wipe the pots of the plants placed outside during cleaning with a moist cloth. Check for signs of pests and disease before returning them inside.

GREENHOUSE CLEAN-UP

1 If you have not already removed the remains of summer shading, do it as soon as possible. Shading washes like this are easy to wipe off with a duster if dry. If left, they will reduce light levels inside the greenhouse.

2 Whether or not summer shading has been used, clean the glass. The easiest way to clean the outside is with a brush or cleaning head on a long handle. Scrub to remove debris. Rinse with clean water.

3 The inside of the glass should be washed with a suitable diluted disinfectant. Using a spray mister is a convenient way to apply the solution. Make sure all traces of algae, dirt and grime are removed.

4 Algae often grow where the panes of glass overlap, an area that also traps dirt. Try squirting a jet of water between the panes, then dislodge the dirt with a thin strip of rigid plastic (a plastic plant label is ideal).

5 Squirt a jet of water between the joints where panes overlap to move the loosened dirt and algae. You may need to repeat the process to dislodge stubborn pieces of dirt. Rinse thoroughly to remove traces of disinfectant.

6 Dirt and soil also accumulate where the glass joins the base, and this can be a breeding ground for pests and diseases. Use a label or a small tool to lift the soil out of the crevice, then douse with a garden disinfectant.

7 Fumigation is a good way to control a number of pests and diseases that may be lurking in nooks and crannies around the greenhouse. Check the manufacturer's instructions to make sure it is suitable for your type and size of greenhouse.

8 It is worth disinfecting the frame and staging, whether or not you fumigate the greenhouse. Use a proprietary garden disinfectant diluted in water and scrub all surfaces thoroughly. Rinse with clean water afterwards.

9 Diseases are easily carried over from one plant to another on old pots and seed trays. When you have time between now and spring, wash them all using a garden disinfectant, scrubbing them thoroughly. Rinse with clean water afterwards.

Winter

A well-planned garden will not be devoid of colour or interest during the winter months, and working outdoors can be a real pleasure. Even when the garden is stripped bare there is much to appreciate in the variety of textures, colours and unexpected scent. The lingering brilliance of autumn fruit and dramatic presence of architectural seedheads are joined by the beautiful bark of many trees and shrubs as well as the bonus of winter flowers. Dramatic skeletal frameworks of fading foliage and seedheads combine with contorted twigs to add charm to the winter garden. Try bold rudbeckias with the thistle-like sea hollies and teasel alongside the skeletal form of hydrangeas for a seasonal highlight after a hoar frost. Nearby, add a few tried and trusted winter bloomers, such as winter jasmine, with its cheerful yellow flowers, and snowdrops, which come in so many different varieties that with careful planning you can have some in flower throughout the winter.

Evergreens are the backbone of the winter garden. Coloured forms, such as this variegated holly, will help light up beds and borders whatever the weather.

The Winter Garden

The onset of winter inevitably means fewer jobs to do in the garden, but it is a good idea to get outdoors whenever the weather is favourable. There is always tidying up to be done, and things like broken fences to be mended. It makes sense to get jobs like this finished before the more severe winter weather makes them less appealing.

Early Winter

If you've been forcing bulbs for winter displays, they should be brought in as they reach the right stage of growth, which is usually a couple of weeks before moving to their flowering position. After flowering they can be planted in the garden to recover.

Early winter is also a good time to assess your garden and make planned improvements. If you decide you need to move an established tree, shrub or climber, there is still time before the worst of the winter weather sets in. New trees and shrubs can also still be planted, and bare-root specimens will be available now.

This is also the time to improve your soil for the next growing season. Nearly all types of soil benefit from the addition of well-rotted organic matter, such as manure and compost. In light, sandy soils it improves retention

Take time out to go through seed catalogues and order supplies of flowers for the coming year.

of moisture and nutrients, as well as adding much-needed nutrients, while in clay soils it opens up the soil structure, introducing air pockets and improving drainage. If your soil is problematic and no plants seem happy, you could try testing for acidity, using a simple kit, or sending a sample to a specialist laboratory for analysis of nutrient levels.

Midwinter

If you made an early start with winter jobs like digging and tidying beds and borders, midwinter is a time mainly for indoor jobs like ordering seeds and plants, writing

Hellebores are indispensable in the winter garden. They thrive in the shadow of deciduous trees and shrubs.

Make early sowings of bedding plants that require a long growing period before they flower.

labels, and designing improvements for the year ahead. These are not unimportant tasks, and by attending to them in good time you are more likely to make the right decisions and have everything ready for late winter and early spring when gardening begins again in earnest. Any spare time should be spent planning for the seasons ahead and going back over the previous year's diary to see where improvements can be made. Take the opportunity to go through catalogues and plant encyclopedias for ideas and draw up a plan of action so that you don't overlook essential tasks during the busy spring months. Don't neglect your garden completely, because there is still plenty to be enjoyed.

It is not too late to protect not-so-hardy plants if you take action immediately. The coldest, windiest and wettest months of the winter still lie ahead, which are the biggest killers of vulnerable garden plants. By midwinter, snow is also a threat in many areas. Light snowfalls are a delight and light up the winter garden scene, but heavy, particularly wet snow can cause serious damage. Shake accumulations of snow from hedges and conifers that tend to catch the snow. If left, the weight will build up and can push them out of shape.

Even in the depths of winter you can propagate a few plants successfully. You can get earlier displays from some flowering plants such as pelargoniums if you sow now, and fibrous-rooted begonias are also worth starting early, if you have the equipment and facilities to grow them on at this time of year. Other plants can be propagated from root cuttings taken now. This is a useful technique for a range of difficult to propagate plants and works best when the plants are dormant. Overwintered chrysanthemums can also be propagated from softwood cuttings as they produce new growth from the old stool. Not only will you get many more plants, but they will be more vigorous and be better able to shrug off pest and disease attacks than if you simply replant the old stools.

Late winter

In some areas late winter can be almost spring-like, especially in a mild winter, but don't be tempted to sow and plant outdoors too soon. If the weather turns very cold, seeds won't germinate, and seedlings and plants may receive such a check to growth that they do not do as well as those sown or planted later. Concentrate your efforts on indoor sowing, but make the most of frames and cloches, too, for early outdoor sowings.

Tuberous begonias for the garden and gloxinias for use indoors or in the greenhouse can be started into growth now. Start begonias in small pots or trays to save space. This will produce well-developed plants that will flower much earlier than tubers planted later direct outside.

Make sure you have placed orders with seed suppliers and nurseries by mail order and from the internet before the spring rush, to ensure you get the varieties you want. Plan your sowing and planting programme carefully so that you do not run out of space and can replace failures along the way. It's also a good idea to work out how many bags of compost (soil mix) you will require and check that you have sufficient pots and other sundries.

Some viburnums flower for a long period over winter, bringing welcome colour and fragrance, usually followed by attractive berries.

Moving trees and shrubs

Autumn and early winter are the best times to move established deciduous trees and shrubs. Wait until mid-spring before you transplant evergreens, including conifers. If your soil is very heavy and poorly drained you might be better off delaying the move of deciduous trees and shrubs until spring, but you will have to keep them well watered throughout the summer. By transplanting now you can be sure that the soil is moist and still warm enough to encourage quick rooting.

Preparing the plants

Always thoroughly soak the plants you are intending to move 24 hours before you want to move them to help prevent the rootball cracking and falling away from the roots. Ideally, move the plants during dull weather or when rain is forecast.

Preparing the new hole

Prepare the planting hole before you start digging up the shrub or tree. Clear the ground of perennial weeds and other debris and improve the water-holding capacity of the soil by incorporating plenty of well-rotted manure or other organic matter.

If shrubs or trees outgrow their allotted space they can be moved while they are dormant during autumn or winter. Get help with large specimens, because the rootball will be very heavy.

MOVING A SHRUB

1 Before you begin to dig up the shrub, make sure that the planting site has been prepared and the hole properly excavated. Water the plant well the day before moving it.

2 Dig a trench around the plant, leaving a large rootball (the size depends on the size of the plant). Sever cleanly any roots that you encounter to release the rootball.

3 Dig under the shrub, cutting through any vertical taproots that hold it in place. Take care that you do not break up the rootball when you are severing thick roots.

Cutting the rootball

The size of the rootball should depend on the size of the tree or shrub you are transplanting. As a rough guide, aim to make the rootball about the same diameter as the spread of a shrub and about one-third the height of a tree. The depth of the rootball will also depend on the soil type: deepest on light, sandy soils; and shallower on heavy clay soils. Small trees and most shrubs are easy to move, especially if they are relatively young. First of all clear the loose soil from around the stem and then cut a vertical slit trench around the shrub to mark the diameter of the rootball and sever any roots that are close to the surface. Make a second slit trench about 30cm (12in) further out and then excavate the soil between the slits to create a flat-bottomed trench as deep as the intended rootball. Undercut the rootball using your spade, severing all the roots you come across until the rootball is completely freed.

With large shrubs and trees you would be better off pruning the roots the year before you want to transplant, by digging the trench around the rootball to sever all the roots near the surface. This will encourage new feeder roots to develop in the soil near to the plant, which will form part of the rootball.

Moving the rootball

Rock the freed rootball over to one side and slide a sheet of strong fabric or plastic underneath. Then rock the plant the other way so that half the fabric can be pulled through. With small rootballs, you can simply tie the fabric around the main stem to hold the soil in place. With large rootballs, you will need to reinforce this with strong string or even rope. Carefully lift or drag the trussed-up rootball to the new planting hole and settle it into place at the same depth it was at previously.

If the rootball is large or you are tackling it on your own, use a short, smooth plank as a slide to help you pull the rootball out of the hole. Then lay the rootball on a piece of thick plastic and drag this to the prepared planting hole. The plastic will slide easily over the soil, grass or paving causing the minimum of damage. To move the rootball up steps use a short plank as a slide.

Check bulbs in store

Don't wait until it is time to plant your tender overwintering bulbs before checking them for rot.

1 Check bulbs, corms and tubers being overwintered in a frost-free place once a month. By eliminating diseased or soft bulbs or corms, you will prevent the rot spreading.

2 If you discover any soft or diseased bulbs in store, discard them and dust the others with a fungicide if you have not already done so.

4 Rock the plant to one side and insert some sacking or plastic as far under the plant as you can. Rock the shrub in the opposite direction and pull the sacking through.

5 Tie the sacking around the main stem. If the combined weight of the plant and rootball is very heavy, get help to move it. Tie a length of wood or metal to the sacking and lift it out.

6 Lower the shrub into the prepared planting hole. Remove the sacking and make sure that the plant is in the right position and at the correct depth. Refill the hole and water well.

Bringing on forced bulbs

Whether your bulbs flower during midwinter, or on any particular date, depends partly on whether you used prepared bulbs in the first place. However, flowering also depends on how cold you keep the bulbs and at what point you bring them out from their resting place into the light and warmth, about 10°C (50°F). After a week or two in these conditions, they can then be moved into their final flowering positions.

Treating bulbs for forcing

It is essential that bulbs placed into plunge beds in autumn are protected from mice and squirrels by covering them with a sheet of chicken wire. Bring in bulbs when they are at the right stage of growth. Hyacinths are the first to show and should be brought into a warmer environment when the flower buds are clearly visible. Forced daffodils should be moved indoors when their leaves are 5–10cm (2–4in) high. Crocuses and tulips should be left until you

can see colour in the breaking flower buds. For longer lasting displays, keep forced bulbs in a cool room in the house and water as necessary. Use hyacinths and hippeastrums (amaryllis) to decorate warmer rooms, because they are more tolerant of higher temperatures.

You can also advance the development of bulbs planted in the garden by covering them with cloches during early winter. They will be ready for cutting several weeks before the rest of the bulbs in the garden.

When flowering is over

It is not worth trying to grow the same hardy bulbs indoors for a second year. Forcing hardy bulbs to flower indoors drains their reserves and the results are almost always disappointing a second time. But there is no need to discard them. Plant them in the garden, where they should gradually recover over a few seasons. If you plan to keep your bulbs for growing in the garden, deadhead them as soon as the display is over. This will avoid energy being wasted on seed production. Do not plant directly into the garden, but acclimatize them gradually by

After forcing, plant out the bulbs so they can gradually recover and provide many years of colourful displays.

placing them in a coldframe or other cool but protected place. Regular watering and a dose of liquid feed will help them recover. In spring, plant the bulbs out in a border or other spot where they can be left undisturbed to grow as a natural group. Some types of bulb may not produce flowers the following season, but probably will do so in subsequent years.

Simple ideas like this single hyacinth and co-ordinated primula often have the most impact.

BRING ON FORCED BULBS

1 Check bowls of bulbs that have been plunged outdoors in beds of sand, peat or grit (to keep them cool and dark while roots develop). When they reach the right stage of development bring them indoors.

2 To protect the bulbs from slugs and other pests, the bowl of planted bulbs can also be put inside a plastic bag before being plunged in the bed outdoors. Open the bag carefully to check their progress.

Keeping hippeastrums

The houseplants popularly but wrongly known as amaryllis are specially treated by the supplier to flower six to eight weeks after they are planted. Many hippeastrums are also sold in flower during the winter. You should be able to keep them so that they flower another year if you follow the advice below. However, they will revert to their normal flowering period of late winter. Cut the flower stalks close to their point of origin once the flowers fade. Keep watered, and feed occasionally. From late spring onwards keep in a greenhouse or conservatory if possible. If you don't have a greenhouse or conservatory, stand the plant outside for the summer. Let the foliage die down in late summer or autumn, then keep the bulbs dry. Start into growth again in late autumn or early winter by gradually increasing watering.

Repotting hippeastrums

Every three or four years, repot using fresh compost – taking care not to disturb the roots. Mix grit into the compost to improve drainage. Replace the surface layer of compost that doesn't contain any roots with fresh each year.

Hippeastrums are specially treated by the supplier to flower in just six to eight weeks after planting, so plant one now for Christmas.

3 If you have kept bulbs in a cool, dark place indoors, such as in a cupboard or loft, check these periodically too. Bring them into the light when the shoots are 2.5–5cm (1–2in) tall.

4 If you sow grass seed on the surface as soon as you bring the bulbs into the light, you should have an attractive carpet of grass by the time they flower to set off the flower display beautifully.

5 Just before the bulbs come into full flower, cut the grass with scissors to a height of about 2.5–5cm (1–2in), to make it look even and neat. Take care not to damage the leaves or flower stems.

Winter protection

You may already have taken action to protect your vulnerable plants from the winter weather, and if you forgot to do so there may well have been some damage by this time. However, in some years the weather can be quite mild during the first part of the winter, and the most severe cold, wind and wet is certainly still to come, so it is well worth while protecting plants now.

Snow and wet

Though a carpeting of snow will benefit plants by insulating the ground from penetrating frosts, as well as bringing undeniable beauty to the garden, heavy snow can cause damage to certain plants. If it accumulates on top of hedges and conifers, it may weigh them down and push them out of shape. You can brush or shake the snow off, or

PROTECTING WINTER HELLEBORE FLOWERS

1 Protect low-growing winter-flowering plants such as *Helleborus niger* with a cloche if you want perfect blooms to cut for indoors. Though the plant is hardy, the flowers tend to become splashed with mud.

2 If you don't have a cloche, improvise with a piece of clear plastic stretched over wire hoops, or a pane of glass supported on bricks. Make sure you weigh down the glass if your garden is exposed so it is not blown away.

prevent it building up in the first place by trimming your hedges in late summer so that they do not have a flat top and by wrapping up conifers with fine-mesh netting or

garden twine. It's also worthwhile replacing the roof netting on fruit cages with wider-mesh netting that will keep the pigeons out but won't collect large amounts of snow that

Although they are perfectly hardy, if you want hellebore flowers for cutting, protect them with cloches in winter to prevent mud splash spoiling the blooms.

might cause the roof of the cage to collapse altogether.

Winter wet can also be a problem for early-flowering plants. Winter-flowering hellebores and early bulbs, such as *Iris unguicularis*, are hardy, but their delicate blooms are often only just above soil level. If you want to cut the flowers to take indoors, covering the plants will reduce mud splashes and keep the blooms clean and in good condition. This will also prevent mischievous birds from stripping the flowers.

Insulating coldframes

Old-fashioned coldframes with brick or timber sides are not as light as modern aluminium and glass or plastic coldframes, but they are

Pruning conifers

Unless they are grown as a restricted form, such as a hedge or topiary, most conifers do not need regular pruning. Any serious pruning of conifers is best carried out while the tree is dormant, before the resinous sap rises and bleeds freely from cut stems. If you want to restrict the size of a conifer, clip it annually with shears or secateurs (pruners), taking care not to prune back into leafless stems because these will not reshoot – exceptions to this are yew (*Taxus*) and cryptomerias, which can safely be cut hard back. Low-growing conifers that have outgrown their allotted space can be reduced in size by removing one or two whole stems, making the cut beneath a newer, shorter shoot on the outside of the plant that will hide it. Variegated conifers occasionally produce an all-green shoot. This problem is called reversion, and the offending shoot should be cut out completely because, if left, these vigorous shoots will eventually dominate the more ornamental foliage.

REMOVING COMPETING LEADERS

1 Where two or more leaders have formed a fork in a conifer, cut away the weaker stem to leave the stronger unpruned. Make a clean cut with a sharp pair of secateurs (pruners) or loppers as close to the main stem as possible.

2 If the remaining leader is not growing vertically, tie a cane to the conifer's main stem. Then tie the bent leader to the cane using soft string for a season until it has assumed the desired upright habit.

warmer. Glass sides let in more light, but also lose heat rapidly. Have the best of both worlds by insulating a glass- or plastic-sided coldframe during the coldest weather, while taking full advantage of the clear sides in spring and summer. Sometimes there are small gaps between the glass and an aluminium frame. This does not matter in hot weather, but for winter warmth it's worth sealing the gaps with draught-proofing strip sold for windows and doors. Insulate the glass sides with sheets of expanded polystyrene (styrofoam). Cut it with a knife or saw. Measure accurately, allowing for the thickness of the material where sheets join at the ends. Push the sheets into place so that they fit tightly.

Coldframes of any kind benefit from having a warm blanket thrown over them on very cold nights. A piece of old carpet is an ideal alternative. Put it in place before the temperature drops, and remember to remove it the next morning unless it remains exceptionally cold. Your plants need light and warmth.

Protecting ponds

During icy weather small water features and ponds can freeze solid. This may damage the container and can kill any aquatic creatures. If you have not already emptied small water features and transferred plants and animals to a temporary winter home under protection, do so now. Even larger ponds can suffer if the cold snap is prolonged. You can help prevent ice forming on the surface by installing a pond heater. If ice is allowed to form it will put pressure on a solid liner and might cause it to crack. You can help to prevent this by floating an inflatable ball on the surface before it freezes to absorb some of the pressure. A complete covering of ice will also trap gases that could poison the pond wildlife, so stand a pan of hot water on the surface to melt a hole. Alternatively, you can use a special electric heater, which will keep a small area free of ice. Do not hammer the ice to break it, since this will send shock waves through the water and could easily kill any fish that are sheltering down at the bottom of the pond.

Propagating in winter

While most plants lie dormant, a few can be propagated in midwinter. One or two summer flowers that need a long growing period before they flower can be raised from seed sown now, and a range of border plants can be propagated from root cuttings. Before you embark on winter propagation, however, make sure you have the right equipment and can maintain sufficiently high temperatures when the young plants are growing on.

Winter sowings

It is too early to sow seeds outdoors, and it is likely to be too soon to sow most tender bedding plants in the greenhouse or on a windowsill, but it is not too soon to sow certain summer flowers that need a long growing period before they flower, such as fibrous-rooted begonias (*Begonia* Semperflorens Group). If in doubt, check the seed packet to see whether a particular flower needs early sowing or not. Because it is difficult to provide the necessary warmth economically at this time of year, especially in a greenhouse, it is best to start the seeds off in a propagator, and move them out once they have germinated. By sowing in pots rather than trays you will be able to germinate more kinds of seeds in your propagator at the same time. Sowing in pots is also sensible if only a few plants are needed, if you are sowing seed of trees and shrubs, for instance.

Pelargoniums need a long growing period before they flower. Sow during winter to be sure of getting flowers by early summer.

TAKING CHRYSANTHEMUM CUTTINGS

1 When your boxes or pots of stools have produced shoots about 5cm (2in) long, it is time to take cuttings.

2 If possible, choose shoots coming directly from the base of the plant. Cut them off close to the base.

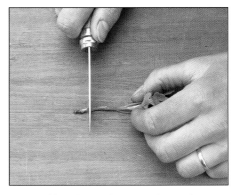

3 Pull off the lowest leaves and trim the ends of the cuttings straight across with a sharp knife.

4 Dip the ends in a rooting hormone. If using a powder, dip the end in water first so that it adheres. Hormone treatment usually improves the rate and speed of rooting, and some preparations contain fungicide.

5 Insert the cuttings around the edge of a pot containing a well-drained compost (soil mix) suitable for cuttings. Make sure that the cuttings are spaced so that the leaves do not touch.

6 If you don't have a propagator, cover the pot with a plastic bag, inflating it to ensure it is not in contact with the leaves. Turn the bag regularly so condensation does not drip on the leaves. Remove after rooting.

TAKING ROOT CUTTINGS

1 If the plant has large, fleshy roots, cut some off close to the main stem or root. You should be able to make several cuttings from one root by dividing it into sections later.

2 Cut each root into pieces about 5cm (2in) long. To help you remember which way up they should be, cut them horizontally at the top and diagonally at the bottom.

3 Fill a pot with a gritty cuttings compost (soil mix) and insert the cuttings using a dibber or pencil. The top of the cutting should be flush with the top of the compost.

4 Some plants, such as border phlox and rock plants like *Primula denticulata*, have thin roots. These can be laid horizontally, and it is not necessary to make sloping cuts to indicate the bottom. Just cut the roots into pieces 2.5–5cm (1–2in) long.

5 Fill a seed tray with a gritty cuttings compost and firm it level tamping it down gently to level the surface and to remove air pockets.

6 Space the cuttings out evenly over the surface, then cover them with a layer of compost. Keep moist, but not too wet, in a coldframe or greenhouse.

Fill pots or trays with a seed sowing compost (soil mix), and gently firm and level it. Sow the seed thinly, and as evenly as possible. Bear in mind that you have to handle the seedlings later, and very close spacing will make this difficult. Most seeds can be sprinkled easily between finger and thumb. Large seeds are best spaced individually. If they are very large, you can insert them into small holes made with a dibber. Most seeds should be covered with a light sprinkling of the same compost. Use a sieve to spread this evenly. Label the seeds.

Check the germination requirements on the seed packet. Some seeds germinate best in light, while others need to be kept dark and so should be covered. To avoid disturbing the evenly distributed seeds, water the pot initially by standing it in shallow water. Remove the pot and let it drain when the surface looks moist. If you don't have a propagator, cover the pot with a sheet of glass or plastic until the seeds germinate.

Taking cuttings

Nearly everyone takes stem cuttings at some time, but surprisingly few gardeners bother with root cuttings. These are likely to be successful only if taken during the dormant season. Several herbaceous perennials can be propagated this way, including acanthus, echinops, gaillardia, border phlox, *Primula denticulata*, *Pulsatilla vulgaris* and *Romneya coulteri*. Select a fleshy root and cut into pieces about 5cm (2in) long making a horizontal cut at the end nearest the plant and a sloping cut furthest away.

Overwintered chrysanthemums can also be increased from softwood cuttings once the old stool, kept frost-free in a greenhouse or coldframe, starts to produce shoots. It is better to raise vigorous young plants from cuttings than to replant the old clump. Encourage the stools to produce the shoots by increasing the temperature to 7°C (45°F).

Making an early start

Get better displays earlier in the season by sowing tender bedding before the spring rush. A heated greenhouse or propagator will enable you to get plants ready for planting out as soon as the weather permits. Late winter is also an ideal time to pot up resting begonia tubers, if you have the heated growing space to keep them warm and safe until the threat of frosts has passed.

Sow early bedding

Late winter is a good time to sow the majority of frost-tender plants used for summer bedding if you have a heated greenhouse, although a few, such as pelargoniums (bedding geraniums) and Semperflorens begonias, are best sown earlier to give them a long period of growth. Because you usually need quite a lot of each kind for bedding, it is normally best to sow the seeds in trays rather than pots. However, you may prefer to use pots for the more difficult seeds that need to be germinated in a propagator, as you can pack more in. Keeping the different varieties separate also allows you to treat them individually.

Early bedding plants, such as this lobelia, are worth sowing early if you have a reliably heated greenhouse and have the protected space to grow them on.

Sowing fine seeds

Very tiny seeds, such as lobelia and begonia, are difficult to handle and to spread evenly. Mix them with a small quantity of silver sand to provide greater bulk, then sprinkle between finger and thumb as you move your hand over the surface of the compost (soil mix). This not only allows you to scatter the seeds evenly but also enables you to see where they are.

Pricking out

Fill the seed trays with a compost recommended for seedlings. Level the surface, then firm it with your fingers or a pressing board.. Prick out a seedling by loosening the soil and lifting up the plant by its seed leaves (the first ones that open, which usually look very different from the true leaves). Make a hole in the compost, deep enough to take most

START TUBERS INTO GROWTH

1 If you are growing your begonias as pot plants, start them off in small pots to save space in the early stages. Loosely fill the pots with a peat-based compost (soil mix), or alternative, intended for seeds or cuttings.

2 If the tubers have small shoots it will be obvious which is the top, otherwise it should be the side with a slight hollow. Lightly press the tuber into the compost. Put in a warm, light place and keep the compost moist.

3 If the begonias are intended for outdoors, perhaps in containers or baskets, start them off in trays instead of pots to save space.

SOWING BEDDING PLANTS

1 Fill a seed tray with seed-sowing compost (soil mix). All-purpose compost could inhibit germination or harm some seedlings. Strike the compost off level with the rim of the tray.

2 Use a presser board (a scrap of wood cut to the right size will usually do the job) to press the compost gently until it is firmed about 1cm (½in) below the rim.

3 Very large seeds can be spaced by hand, but most medium-sized seeds are easily scattered with a folded piece of stiff paper. Tap it with a finger as you move it over the surface.

4 Unless the packet advises not to cover the seeds (a few require light to germinate while others do better in light), cover them by sifting more of the seed compost over the top to provide an even layer.

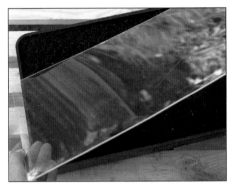

5 Unless you are placing the tray in a propagator, cover it with a sheet of glass, or place it in a plastic bag. Turn the glass over or the bag inside out regularly to prevent condensation drips.

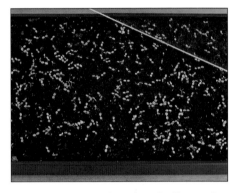

6 Remove any covering when the first seeds start to germinate. If you don't, the seedlings may succumb to disease. It may be possible to reduce the amount of warmth after germination, but good light is always essential.

Tuberous-rooted begonias can be started off in the greenhouse now for a prolonged summer display.

of the roots without curling them. Gently firm the compost round the roots. To help produce an evenly spaced box of plants, first prick out a row along the end and one side. When you have this spacing right, fill in the rest of the tray. The exact spacing will depend on the type of plant that you are pricking out. Large seeds need more space than small ones. You may find it more convenient to use a modular tray system. Although it is more expensive and takes up more room on the bench, it does makes spacing easier, and there is less root disturbance when the plants are eventually put in the garden.

Start off begonia and gloxinia tubers

Tuberous-rooted begonias can be grown as pot plants or in the garden and it is well worth starting them into growth now in the greenhouse. This way you will have well-developed plants to put in the garden that will flower much earlier than if the tubers were planted directly into the soil later on.

Gloxinias, which are suitable only for cultivation in the home or greenhouse, should also be started into growth now. If they are grown as pot plants you can plant them in their final 13–15cm (5–6in) pots. The hairy side is the one to press into the compost (soil mix).

Jobs in brief

No matter how experienced you are at gardening it is very easy to overlook something or forget to carry out an essential task at the correct time. Use the following checklists to help you plan ahead and if you require more details, turn to the relevant page within the book to find a complete description of each task, often accompanied by step-by-step photographs. These seasonal checklists will also help you prioritize your gardening activities when time is short such as during the busy spring months. The exact timing of each garden task should not be determined by the calendar, but by the local weather and soil conditions in your garden. For example, you may have to delay early sowings and planting outside for several weeks if winter extends into spring or if you have heavy soil or garden on an exposed plot. Use a soil thermometer to check soil temperatures before you sow and plant and make sure that all plants are thoroughly hardened off before they are positioned outside.

A busy gardener needs to plan ahead to make best use of time, space and money available. The following checklists should help.

SPRING

In cold regions the weather can still be icy in early spring, but in mild climates you can make a start on many outdoor jobs. If sowing or planting outdoors, bear in mind that soil temperature as well as air temperature is important. Few seeds will germinate if the soil temperature is below 7°C (45°F), so use a soil thermometer to check before you sow.

The garden looks colourful again by mid-spring, seedlings and cuttings are growing fast, and outdoor sowing and planting can begin in earnest. Heavy showers are commonplace which can wash out outdoor sowings and emerging rows of seedlings, so it's important to have a stack of cloches to provide some temporary cover.

The weather in late spring can be very unpredictable, and it often seems that summer has already arrived, but it's important not to plant out any frost-tender plants too early. Watching the weather forecasts and observing when summer bedding is planted out in local public parks – since these gardeners should have plenty of experience and local knowledge – can help you assess the risks.

SPRING JOBS IN BRIEF

Early Spring
- [ ] Sow hardy annuals
- [ ] Create new flower beds
- [ ] Divide perennials
- [ ] Plant herbaceous plants
- [ ] Plant shrubs and trees
- [ ] Prune shrubs and trees
- [ ] Prune roses and climbers
- [ ] Prepare the ground for a new lawn
- [ ] Make a new lawn

Mid-spring
- [ ] Stake herbaceous plants
- [ ] Create a mowing strip
- [ ] Sow wildflowers
- [ ] Make a new pond
- [ ] Make and plant a bog garden
- [ ] Make a pebble fountain
- [ ] Make and plant a rock garden
- [ ] Plant a hanging basket

Late Spring
- [ ] Sow biennials and hardy perennials
- [ ] Improve flowering displays by pinching out, feeding, weeding, mulching and deadheading
- [ ] Improve trees and shrubs by planting a climber next to an established shrub
- [ ] Plant marginal aquatics in ponds
- [ ] Plant a waterlily
- [ ] Plant a shrub in a tub
- [ ] Plant a patio
- [ ] Fill cracks and crevices in the patio
- [ ] Make an ivy standard
- [ ] Plant a trough with alpines

When planting a rootballed tree or shrub, carefully untie the wrapping and slide it into the hole. Always try to avoid any disturbance of the ball of soil around the roots.

Support clump-forming perennials using proprietary hoops with adjustable legs. Stake tall flowering stems by tying them to a cane that is shorter than the eventual height of the plant and hidden from sight behind the stem.

When planting marginal plants water first to remove any air pockets in the compost. Then carefully place on the shelf at the edge of the pool so that the container is covered by 3–5cm (1–2in) of water.

PLANTS AT THEIR BEST

Early Spring

Camellia (shrub)
Chaenomeles (wall shrub)
Clematis alpina
  (climber)
Cornus mas (shrub)
Crocus (bulb)
Eranthis hyemalis
  (bulb)
Garrya elliptica (shrub)
Helleborus orientalis
  (herbaceous)
Iris reticulata (bulb)
Mahonia (shrub)
Pulmonaria (herbaceous)
Salix (shrub)
Spirea thunbergia (shrub)
Tulipa kaufmanniana (bulb)

Pure white, star-shaped flowers of *Magnolia stellata* are sometimes flushed with pink.

Dicentra formosa produces wonderful arching stems of pink heart-shaped flowers.

Mid-spring

Bellis (biennial)
Dicentra (herbaceous)
Forsythia (shrub)
Hyacinthoides (bulb)
Hyacinthus (bulb)
Kerria (shrub)
Magnolia × soulangiana (tree)
Magnolia stellata (shrub)
Muscari armeniacum (bulb)
Narcissus (bulb)
Prunus 'Kwanzan' (tree)
Pulsatilla vulgaris (rock
  plant)
Ribes sanguineum (shrub)
Tulipa, various (bulb)

Wisteria sinensis is covered in pendant sprays of fragrant, pea-like, late spring flowers.

Late Spring

Aubrieta (rock plant)
Bergenia (non-woody
  evergreen)
Choisya ternata (shrub)
Clematis montana (shrubby
  climber)
Crataegus (tree)
Cytisus, various (shrub)
Erysimum (biennial)
Fritillaria (bulb)
Genista (shrub)
Laburnum (tree)
Malus (tree)
Paeonia (herbaceous
  and shrub)
Phlox subulata
  (rock plant)
Pulsatilla vulgaris
  (rock plant)
Rhododendron, various
  (shrub)
Saxifraga, various
  (rock plant)
Syringa (shrub)
Tulipa, various (bulb)
Wisteria (shrubby
  climber)

SUMMER

The garden will be full of colour in early summer, and you should have time to relax a little and reap the rewards of all your efforts over the past few months. You can enjoy abundant displays of flowers. There are still plenty of maintenance tasks, however: the lawn will be growing strongly, as will weeds, so these need to be kept under control. Many pests and diseases will be active at this time of year, too: keep a close eye out for any attacks, and whenever possible, take preventative action – such as putting up barriers – before any serious damage occurs.

Midsummer is mainly a time to enjoy your garden, rather than do a lot of strenuous work in it. Most things are already sown or planted, and the emphasis is on weeding and watering. Regular deadheading will keep plants looking tidy and flowering well. If you go away, make sure your plants will not run short of water, especially those in containers.

We can usually expect some hot, dry weather in late summer, and it's a good time to enjoy garden parties and barbecues, since there should be plenty of things to admire in the garden.

SUMMER JOBS IN BRIEF

Early Summer
- [ ] Deadhead flowers
- [ ] Prune shrubs
- [ ] Renovate neglected shrubs
- [ ] Plant a window box
- [ ] Plant up tubs and patio pots

Midsummer
- [ ] Take semi-ripe cuttings
- [ ] Propagate bulbs, such as lilies and flag irises
- [ ] Save flower seed
- [ ] Look after the pond by clearing weeds, protecting fish and tidying up plants
- [ ] Layer shrubs and carnations

Late Summer
- [ ] Plant bulbs for spring
- [ ] Care for dahlias and chrysanthemums
- [ ] Trim hedges
- [ ] Trim groundcover to encourage the plants to grow more densely with fewer straggly stems
- [ ] Cut back shoots wherever reversion has begun

Choose a tall or bold plant for the centre of a summer container and surround it with bushy plants with contrasting leaf shapes and complementary flower colour (top). Water thoroughly after planting (above).

Take semi-ripe cuttings. Choose shoots that are almost fully grown. Trim the bottom of the cutting just below a leaf joint, then strip the lower leaves from each cutting (above).

Remove any kind of litter or rubbish that is lurking amongst the groundcover. Most groundcover will look better if it is trimmed back at least once a year.

PLANTS AT THEIR BEST

Herbaceous peonies make excellent specimen plants for the middle of a border in full sun or partial shade.

Early Summer

Alchemilla mollis (herbaceous)
Allium (bulb)
Buddleja globosa (shrub)
Calendula (hardy annual)
Choisya ternata (shrub)
Cistus (shrub)
Clematis montana (climber)
Dianthus (perennial and biennial)
Digitalis (biennial)
Genista (shrub)
Geranium (herbaceous)
Godetia (hardy annual)
Iris germanica hybrids (bulb)
Laburnum (tree)
Lupinus (herbaceous)
Malus (tree)
Philadelphus (shrub)
Rosa (most types of rose)
Weigela (shrub)

'Bronwen North' is a delightful turkscap lily that bears its colourful flowers in midsummer.

Midsummer

Alchemilla mollis (herbaceous)
Althaea (herbaceous)
Astilbe (herbaceous)
Cistus (shrub)
Clematis, some (shrubby climber)
Dianthus (carnations and pinks)
Digitalis (biennial)
Geranium (herbaceous)
Hardy annuals (many)

Helianthemum (shrub)
Hydrangea (shrub)
Hypericum (shrub)
Kniphofia (herbaceous)
Lavandula (shrub)
Lilium (bulb)
Potentilla (shrub)
Rosa (most types of rose)
Summer bedding
Verbascum (herbaceous)

Late Summer

Dahlia (bulb)
Erigeron (herbaceous)
Fuchsia (shrub)
Helenium (herbaceous)
Hibiscus syriacus (shrub)
Hypericum (shrub)
Lavatera (shrub)
Romneya (shrub)
Verbascum (herbaceous)

Add a flamboyant touch to your late summer garden with the delicate paper petals of *Romneya coulteri*.

AUTUMN

The weather in early autumn is still warm enough to make outdoor gardening a comfortable experience, and although the vibrant flowers of summer may be gone, there are plenty of delights to be enjoyed in the form of flaming foliage and late-flowering gems such as chrysanthemums and nerines. Apart from bulb planting, and protecting frost-tender plants, there are few really pressing jobs at this time of year. The weather is unpredictable during mid-autumn and it's crucial to keep an eye on the forecasts and take action whenever necessary to protect vulnerable plants. Fallen leaves will be plentiful, and these should be cleared away regularly.

It's important to protect vulnerable plants in late autumn, before winter sets in. Any that haven't already been moved to a frost-free place, or covered with a suitable protection, should be attended to as necessary. Now is the perfect time to plant deciduous shrubs and trees – bare-rooted specimens are now available, and container-grown plants, though they can be planted at any time, are best planted now.

EARLY AUTUMN JOBS IN BRIEF

Early Autumn
- [ ] Clear summer bedding
- [ ] Lift and store gladioli and other tender bulbs, corms and tubers
- [ ] Plant lilies for the summer
- [ ] Store garden canes – extend their life by cleaning and preserving them, and storing in a dry place rather than leaving them exposed in the garden
- [ ] Remove thatch and moss from the lawn
- [ ] Feed and weed the lawn
- [ ] Collect leaves, keeping those shed by deciduous trees and shrubs as they make good leafmould once rotted down
- [ ] Make any necessary lawn repairs
- [ ] Plant bulbs for a spring-flowering window box
- [ ] Plant spring containers

Mid-autumn
- [ ] Naturalize bulbs in grass and under the canopy of trees
- [ ] Save tender bulbs for next year
- [ ] Plant new shrubs and hedges
- [ ] Prune rambling roses
- [ ] Cover the pond with fine-mesh netting to prevent leaves falling into it
- [ ] Protect pond pumps
- [ ] Overwinter tender aquatics
- [ ] Protect tender plants in containers by moving them into the greenhouse or conservatory where they can be kept frost-free
- [ ] Provide insulation for borderline-hardy perennials in borders
- [ ] Overwinter tender perennials indoors, cutting plants back ready to take cuttings in spring

Late Autumn
- [ ] Lift and protect chrysanthemums
- [ ] Pot up winter aconites
- [ ] Weed and apply a generous amount of mulch to beds
- [ ] Lift tender bulbs and pot them up or overwinter them in boxes somewhere frost-free
- [ ] Cut back dying foliage on herbaceous perennials
- [ ] Plant trees, and stake them if they are tall
- [ ] Take hardwood shrub cuttings
- [ ] Protect vulnerable shrubs [ ] Protect newly planted evergreens from wind damage
- [ ] Cover alpines that need protection from winter wet with a pane of glass
- [ ] Protect plants from the cold by wrapping them in bubble wrap

Tender bulbs, such as gladioli, should be lifted now and stored in a frost-free place. Loosen the soil with a spade or fork before attempting to lift the plants.

Prepare your pond for winter by clearing fallen leaves as well as overgrown submerged oxygenating plants, that will clog the pond.

Insert three stakes around a shrub being protected, then wrap a plastic sheet or several layers of garden fleece around the edge. Peg down the bottom and staple the sides.

PLANTS AT THEIR BEST

Early Autumn

Anemone x hybrida (herbaceous)
Aster novae-angliae (herbaceous)
Aster novi-belgii (herbaceous)
Chrysanthemum, early flowering garden type (herbaceous)
Dahlia
Hibiscus syriacus (shrub)
Hydrangea (shrub)
Lavatera (shrub)
Nerine bowdenii (bulb)
Pyracantha, berries (shrub)
Rudbeckia (herbaceous)
Sedum spectabile (herbaceous)
Solidago (herbaceous)
Sorbus, berries (tree)
Sternbergia lutea (bulb)

Japanese anemones give a reliable display of elegant blooms throughout the autumn.

Mid-autumn

Acer, colourful foliage (tree/shrub)
Berberis, colourful foliage and berries (shrub)
Cotoneaster, berries (shrub)
Fothergilla, colourful foliage (shrub)
Gentiana sino-ornata (alpine)
Liriope muscari (herbaceous)
Pernettya, berries (shrub)
Pyracantha, berries (shrub)
Schizostylis coccinea (herbaceous)

Chrysanthemum 'Primrose Allouise' is an outdoor variety that bears its superb blooms during the early autumn.

Late Autumn

Acer, colourful foliage (tree/shrub)
Aster novi-belgii (herbaceous)
Berberis, colourful foliage and berries (shrub)
Fothergilla, colourful foliage (shrub)
Liriope muscari (herbaceous)
Parthenocissus, colourful foliage (climber)
Pernettya, berries (shrub)
Pyracantha, berries (shrub)
Schizostylis coccinea (herbaceous)

The eye-catching kaffir lily offers a late splash of stunning colour when most other flowers are past their best.

WINTER

In early winter, before the weather gets too cold, it's a good idea to spend some time tidying up the garden. You can see the garden framework clearly now, which should give you ideas for future improvements. If the garden looks really drab, think about which plants you can introduce to make it more appealing next winter: there are lots of wonderful berrying and winter-flowering plants to choose from. And if you don't know much about your soil, it may be useful to get a soil testing kit.

If you made an early start with winter jobs like digging and tidying beds and borders, midwinter is a time mainly for indoor jobs like ordering seeds and plants, writing labels, and designing improvements for the year ahead. These are not unimportant tasks, and by attending to them in good time you are more likely to make the right decisions and have everything ready for late winter.

In late winter you can enjoy the sight of the emerging bulbs and early-flowering shrubs. Some sowings can be made in the greenhouse or in propagators, but don't be in a hurry to sow or plant outdoors – seeds sown later will usually overtake the early-sown plants, which will struggle in cold conditions.

WINTER JOBS IN BRIEF

Early Winter
- ☐ Check bulbs, corms and tubers in store
- ☐ Move deciduous trees and shrubs, making sure that the planting site has been prepared and the hole properly excavated first
- ☐ Bring forced bulbs into the greenhouse when they are at the right stage of growth

Midwinter
- ☐ Protect winter hellebore flowers with a cloche
- ☐ Insulate coldframes for extra protection in the cold weather with sheets of expanded polystyrene (styrofoam)
- ☐ Put a warm blanket or piece of old carpet over the coldframe at night but remember to remove it in the morning
- ☐ Prune conifers
- ☐ Prevent ponds freezing over
- ☐ Take root cuttings of herbaceous perennials
- ☐ Sow bedding plants in the greenhouse

Late Winter
- ☐ Service your mower or have it done professionally
- ☐ Order seeds, bulbs and plants for the coming season
- ☐ Tidy up the rock garden, and apply fresh stone chippings
- ☐ Check labels on shrubs and border plants and renew them if you think it is necessary
- ☐ Prick out seedlings planted earlier in the greenhouse

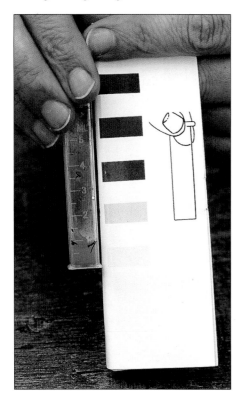

If plants don't seem to perform very well in your garden, try testing the soil with a simple kit that measures acidity/alkalinity or nutrient levels.

Protect low-growing winter-flowering plants such as *Helleborus niger* with a cloche if you want perfect blooms to cut for indoors. The plant is hardy but the flowers tend to become splashed and damaged by the weather.

Very large seeds can be spaced by hand, but most medium-sized seeds are easily scattered with a folded piece of stiff paper. Tap it with a finger as you move it over the surface.

PLANTS AT THEIR BEST

Early Winter

Chimonanthus praecox (shrub)
Erica carnea (shrub)
Erica × darleyensis (shrub)
Hamamelis mollis (shrub)
Ilex, berries (shrub/tree)
Iris unguicularis (syn. *I. stylosa*)
  (herbaceous)
Jasminum nudiflorum (wall shrub)
Liriope muscari (herbaceous)
Mahonia bealei (shrub)
Mahonia 'Charity' (shrub)
Pernettya, berries (shrub)
Prunus × subhirtella 'Autumnalis' (tree)
Pyracantha, berries (shrub)
Sarcococca (shrub)
Viburnum × bodnantense (shrub)
Viburnum farreri (shrub)

Midwinter

Chimonanthus praecox (shrub)
Eranthis hyemalis (bulb)
Erica carnea (shrub)
Erica × darleyensis (shrub)
Galanthus nivalis (bulb)
Garrya elliptica (shrub)
Hamamelis mollis (shrub)
Iris unguicularis (syn. *I. stylosa*)
  (herbaceous)

Ilex, berries (tree/shrub)
Jasminum nudiflorum (wall shrub)
Lonicera fragrantissima (shrub)
Prunus × subhirtella 'Autumnalis' (tree)
Sarcococca (shrub)
Viburnum × bodnantense (shrub)
Viburnum farreri (syn. *V. fragrans*)
  (shrub)
Viburnum tinus (shrub)

Late Winter

Crocus (bulb)
Daphne mezereum (shrub)
Eranthis hyemalis (bulb)
Erica carnea (shrub)
Erica × darleyensis (shrub)
Galanthus nivalis (bulb)
Garrya elliptica (shrub)
Helleborus niger (herbaceous)
Helleborus orientalis (herbaceous)
Iris reticulata (bulb)
Iris unguicularis (syn. *I. stylosa*)
  (herbaceous)
Jasminum nudiflorum (wall shrub)
Muscari armeniacum (bulb)
Prunus cerasifera (tree)
Prunus × subhirtella 'Autumnalis' (tree)
Sarcococca (shrub)
Viburnum × bodnantense (shrub)
Viburnum tinus (shrub)

(Above) Sweet box, *Sarcococca confusa*, bears fragrant white flowers in winter, followed by glossy black berries.

(Left) *Viburnum × bodnantense* bears fragrant clusters of pink flowers.

Eranthis hyemalis (far left) will light up the border under the bare branches of trees and shrubs.

Glossary

Annual A plant that grows from seed, flowers, sets seed and dies in one year.

Aquatic A plant that lives in water: it can be completely submerged, floating or live with its roots in the water.

Bare-root A plant sold with no soil or compost around the roots. They are dug up from the nursery field and must be planted immediately.

Bedding plant A plant that is raised for use in a temporary garden display; spring, summer and winter types are available.

Biennial A plant that grows from seed to form a small plant in the first year, flowers and sets seed in the following year, and then dies.

Biological control The use of a pest's natural enemies to control its numbers in the garden or greenhouse.

Bog garden An area of ground that remains permanently wet and is used to grow bog plants

Capillary matting An absorbent material that holds a lot of water on which containers are placed and from which they can draw all the moisture they need.

Certified stock Plants that have been inspected and declared free of specific pests and diseases.

Cloche A small structure made from glass, clear plastic or polythene that is used to warm small areas of soil or protect vulnerable plants.

Compost (soil mix) A mixture that is used for growing plants in containers. It can be loam-based or peat-based. Peat-free versions are now available based on coir, composted bark or other organic waste material.

Compost, garden A material that has been produced from the decomposition of organic waste material in a compost bin or heap. Useful as a soil improver or planting mixture.

Crop covers Various porous materials that are used to protect plants or crops. Horticultural fleece protects plants from frost and flying insect pests; insect-proof mesh is a well-ventilated fabric, ideal for keeping out insects throughout the summer, but offers no frost protection.

Cultivate To prepare the land and soil for growing crops.

Deadhead To remove spent flowers to tidy the display, prevent the formation of seeds and improve future flowering.

Fleece *see* Crop covers

Grafted plant A plant that has been attached on to the rootstock of another variety. Trees, especially fruit trees, are often grafted on to dwarfing rootstocks, while ornamental plants may be grafted on to a more vigorous variety.

Groundcover plants These are densely growing, mat-forming plants that can be used to cover the ground with foliage to prevent weeds germinating.

Hardening off A method of gradually weaning a plant from the conditions inside to those outside without causing a check to growth.

Hardiness The amount of cold a type of plant is able to withstand. Hardy plants can tolerate frost; half-hardy and tender plants cannot.

Herbaceous plants Plants that produce sappy, green, non-woody growth. Herbaceous perennials die down in winter, but re-grow from basal shoots the following spring.

Horticultural fleece *see* Crop covers.

Humus The organic residue of decayed organic matter found in soil. It improves soil fertility.

Insect-proof mesh *see* Crop covers.

Leafmould A material that has been produced from the decomposition of leaves in a bin or heap. Useful as a soil improver or planting mixture.

Mulch A material that is laid on the surface of the soil to prevent moisture loss through evaporation and to suppress weed growth. A mulch can be loose and organic, such as composted bark or garden compost, loose and inorganic, such as gravel, or a fabric, such as mulch matting or landscape fabric.

Perennial A plant that lives for more than two years. The term is usually applied to a hardy non-woody plant (*see* Herbaceous). A tender perennial is a non-woody plant that cannot tolerate frost.

Pricking out The spacing of seedlings while still small so that they have room to develop and grow on.

Rootball A mass of roots and compost that holds together when a plant is removed from its container.

Runner A horizontal shoot that spreads out from the plant roots and forms another plant.

Sucker A shoot that arises from the roots underground. The term is usually applied to shoots from the rootstock of a grafted plant that has undesirable characteristics.

Transplanting The transfer of seedlings or young plants from a nursery bed where they were sown to their final growing position.

Windbreak A hedge, fence, wall or fabric that is used to filter the wind and therefore reduce the damage that it may cause.

Tulips and double daisies

Index

Acknowledgements

The publisher would like to thank Peter McHoy for his permission to use the following photographs: p30 all pics, p56 all pics, p57 all bottom pics, p75tr, tc, cr, cl, p86t, cl, cr, bl, br, p87c, p100t, p108br, bc, p109 bl, bc, br.

Photographs: Peter Anderson, Jonathan Buckley, Sarah Cuttle, Paul Forrester, John Freeman, Michelle Garrett, Jacqui Hurit, Debbie Patterson and Steven Wooster.